100

Ships and Planes

That Shaped World History

William Caper

D1378274

A Bluewood Book

This edition produced and published
by Bluewood Books
A Division of The Siyeh Group, Inc.,
P.O. Box 689
San Mateo, CA 94401

ISBN 0-912517-38-7

Printed in U.S.A.
10, 9, 8, 7, 6, 5, 4, 3, 2, 1

Editor: Tony Napoli
Editorial Assistance: Jill Fox
Indexer: Kathy Paparchontis
Designer: Kevin Harris

Key to cover illustration:
   Clockwise, starting from top left:
the Glamorous Glennis, the Great
Harry, the Spirit of St. Louis, the
Monitor and the Merrimack, the
Titanic, the B-2 Stealth, and the
Concorde in the center.

About the Author:
   William Caper was born in
New York City. He holds a degree
from Brooklyn College, where he
majored in literature. He has been a
free-lance writer for more than 20
years, and is the author of *Whoopi
Goldberg: Comedian and Screen Star*
(Enslow Publishers, 1999). His interests
are history, literature, traveling, and
film. He currently lives in San
Francisco with his wife, Erin, and dog,
Face.

Picture Acknowledgements: Aero
Spacelines: 97; Air France: 99;
American Airlines: 69; Bluewood
Archives: 11, 13, 14, 16, 17, 18, 28,
29, 31, 36, 41, 44, 66; Boeing
Company: 92, 101, 103, 105, 106;
British Museum: 12, 33, 70, 95, 98;
Burlingame Public Library 40;
Compagnie Generale Maritime: 67;
Cunard Line: 51, 68, 73; Hughes
Aircraft: 88; Imperial War Museum:
55, 57, 62, 63, 74, 78, 83; KLM: 58;
Library of Congress: 24, 39, 47, 60,
61, 79; Lockheed Corporation: 75;
Mariners Museum: 30, 32, 89;
McDonald Douglas: 100; Museum of
Hamburg: 49; National Archives: 45,
64, 65, 71, 80, 104; National Liberty
Ship Memorial 84; National Maritime
Museum: 15, 19, 20, 21, 23, 25, 27,
34, 35, 37, 42, 46, 54; National
Oceanic and Atmospheric
Administration: 104; NYPL: 10;
Potomac Association: 72; Royal Navy:
50, 84; Russian Imperial Navy: 48;
San Mateo Public Library: 9; U.S. Air
Force: 52, 59, 76, 81, 82, 85, 87,
90, 91, 96; U.S. Navy: 22, 26, 38,
43, 53, 56, 77, 86, 93, 94, 102,
107; Universitetets Oldsaksamling,
Oslo: 8.

TABLE OF CONTENTS

15.
10. 16.18.
1.   2.   3. 4. 5. 6. 7. 8. 9. 11.12. 13.14. 17.19.

A.D. 900   **1800**

TABLE OF CONTENTS

41.
42.
43.
37.   **44.** **48.**
38.   **45.** **49.**

20.   **23.** **25.**   **30.**   **33.**   **39.** **40.** **46.** **50.**
21. 22.   **24.** **26.** **27.** **28.** **29.** **31. 32. 34.** **35.** **36.**   **47.** **51.**

1801   **1920**

TABLE OF CONTENTS

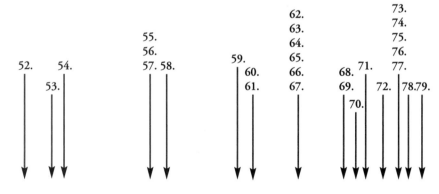

1921   1945

TABLE OF CONTENTS

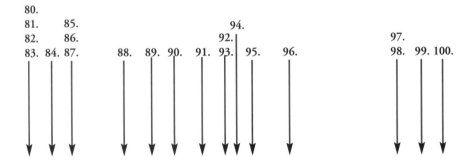

1946   2000

INTRODUCTION

The development of ships and planes represents many things: exploration, trade and commerce, war, and adventurous travel to faraway places. They are an integral part of human history, and symbolize the great technological achievements humans have made over the past several hundred years.

Even the first watercraft, which were simply floating logs, showed our ability to evolve, for it took intelligence and logic to realize that if a log can float, a person might use that log to travel over water. As boats developed, so did civilizations and cultures. People living in cities hundreds, then thousands, of miles apart could trade goods and share knowledge. It is no coincidence that many of the world's major cities are located near oceans or rivers.

For centuries, ships have had a major impact on the development of nations. They helped redistribute the world's peoples. The Pilgrims' ship *Mayflower*, the English clipper ship *Cutty Sark*, and the German ocean liner *Auguste Victoria* were just three of the countless vessels that brought immigrants to new countries. Other vessels helped new, small communities grow into major population areas by transporting goods and services across large bodies of water.

Over the years, ships have also been an essential element of warfare—from the early 17th century naval warships to the late 20th century nuclear-powered aircraft carriers. Boats also bring people pleasure. Vessels of all sizes, from the sleek racing yacht *America* to elegant floating palaces like the *Queen Elizabeth 2*, offer the sheer fun and thrill of being on the open water.

Sometimes the very name of a vessel conjures up a powerful vision. The *Half Moon, Golden Hind*, and *Kon-Tiki* are linked with exploration, discovery, and adventure. The *Titanic* is associated with tragedy. The *Normandie, Queen Mary*, and *Queen Elizabeth* are synonymous with the romance of a bygone era. The *Victory,*

Lusitania, Arizona, and *Enterprise* represent turning points in history.

The invention of the airplane reflects our ability to transcend ourselves even more than the development of ships. People have dreamed of flying as far back as the ancient Greeks. After thousands of years, on a strip of beach in North Carolina, the Wright Brothers biplane *Flyer* made this dream a reality.

Like ships, airplanes have been vital to exploration, trade, war, and peace. Unlike ships, they are a wholly 20th-century phenomenon. All the progress in powered flight—from the Wright brothers at Kitty Hawk, and Charles Lindbergh's solo crossing of the Atlantic in the *Spirit of St. Louis,* to the DC-3, *Glamorous Glennis* and the Concorde—was made in the 20th century.

This book tells the stories of 100 ships and planes that have shaped history. Some entries describe vessels and aircraft that have played important roles in historic events. Others describe the development of a particular type of ship or plane that marked a major step forward in the advancement of the technology of seagoing vessels and powered aircraft. In both instances you'll learn many interesting facts, not only about the ships and planes themselves, but about the fascinating men and women who developed, built, captained, and piloted them.

This book also includes a glossary of nearly 100 nautical and aeronautical terms, some of which may already be familiar to those readers who have spent time learning about ships and planes elsewhere. All glossary terms are in boldface type the first time they appear in an entry.

Ships and planes are more than a way of traveling from one place to another. They represent our growth and progress over the centuries. So this book is a look into the distant past, as well as a journey to the edge of the 21st century. It is the story of the ability, desire, and determination of the human race to use its knowledge and technology to reach the greatest heights.

The Oseberg Ship

Fierce warriors on land, the Vikings were also master seamen who ranged far from their home ports in Scandinavia. They even sailed their sturdy ships to the New World. The famed Viking Leif Ericson reached North America nearly 500 years before Christopher Columbus and named the region Vinland.

The Vikings took to the sea in longships, called snake or dragon ships. These long narrow vessels were **clinker-built**. They had large **bow** and **stern** posts that were usually curled into a spiral, or elaborately carved as a figure meant to honor the gods and please spirits of the seas. Longships were of shallow **draught** so they could navigate rivers, could be rowed when there was no wind, and could be easily beached on shore. They had a low **freeboard** that could be increased by attaching shields to the side of the ship to prevent water from washing over the side. Instead of a permanent deck, they had loose boards, with equipment or cargo stored below.

One square sail hung from a short single mast that was usually **amidships**. These ves-

sels had only basic **backstays**. Because they did not carry shrouds, they sailed with the wind behind them. With no support from shrouds, the masts could not take the strain of the wind hitting the sail on an angle.

The ship was steered with a tiller that was attached to a short oar. This oar was mounted on the right side of the boat, and became known as the steering board. Over time, the right side of any ship became the **starboard** side.

Several Viking boats still exist. One of the most well known is the Oseberg Ship, which dates from about A.D. 900. The Oseberg Ship was found in 1904, near Tonsberg, Norway. Made of strong oak, with 12 planks on each side, it is 70 feet long and almost 17 feet across the **beam**. The boat carried 30 oars and a sail mounted on its one mast. Its well-designed steering board extended deeply into the water and was connected to a short tiller. Later ships reached lengths of 300 feet and carried as many as 60 oars. When the Oseberg Ship was discovered, the skeleton of a Viking Queen was found inside, which was not a surprising fact since the Vikings were known for giving their dead warriors and members of royalty glorious funerals at sea.

Today, the Oseberg Ship is on display at the Vikingskiphuset Museum in Oslo, Norway.

2. Christopher of the Tower
1340

The Vikings relied on their longships for war. These boats were designed to transport raiding parties along a coast or up a river, not to make voyages across the open sea. As trade developed between nations, a different kind of ship was needed to carry large amounts of goods because longships did not have the cargo capacity demanded of vessels engaged in commerce. During the 14th century, shipbuilders began experimenting with new designs and the longship evolved into the round ship.

Built to carry cargo below deck and heavy equipment on deck, round ships were wider than longships and had a deeper **draught**. Instead of the longships' loose floor boards, the round ships had thick permanent deck planks; the longships' towering stem and stern posts were replaced with **forecastles,** toward the front of the ship, and **sterncastles** toward the rear. When they were first introduced, these small houselike structures held archers who fired on enemy ships and on boarders who were trying to capture a ship. Early castle structures were not very solid, but over time they were built better and became increasingly elaborate. Over the years, they came to be used as quarters for the crew.

Masts increased in size and diameter, becoming stronger so they could carry bigger sails. As they grew in size, masts were stepped, or attached, to the ship by fitting them into special supports. Atop these masts were crow's nests, platforms where lookouts kept watch for land, other ships, and enemy forces. During battle, crow's nests were especially useful. From here, bowmen and spearmen could fire on enemies, and soldiers could drop heavy stones on boarders.

At first, round ships were **clinker-built** and single-masted with one square sail. Later, a large **spar** called a **bowsprit** was added, extending over the front of the vessel at an angle. The bowsprit gives additional support to the mast and can carry additional sails. As round ships became more advanced, the steering oar developed into a rudder that was mounted on the vessel's **stern-post**.

During the Hundred Years' War between England and France (1337–1453), the English fleet of Edward III included the round ship *Christopher of the Tower,* one of the first ships to carry deck-mounted guns. On June 24, 1340, some 150 English ships engaged nearly 200 French ships in the harbor of Sluys, in the Netherlands. With its superior firepower, *Christopher of the Tower* was instrumental in defeating the French. This was the first important battle of the Hundred Years' War, and the victory gave Britain control of the English Channel.

Round ships remained in wide use throughout Europe until the 15th century. In the Mediterranean, they were known as *dromons.* In northern European and Atlantic waters, they were called *cogs.*

14th century cogs in action

9

3. Santa María / Niña / Pinta
1492

Three of the most famous ships in history are the vessels that carried Christopher Columbus to the New World in 1492—the *Niña*, the *Pinta* and the *Santa María*.

No plans or drawings of the *Santa María*, *Niña* or *Pinta* exist, so we don't know exactly what they looked like. However, some information about all three vessels is part of the historical record.

It is believed the *Santa María* was a 100-ton **caravel**. Early caravels had two masts rigged with **lateens**. Lateen-rigged ships had narrow, triangular sails on a long yard that was usually set at a large forward angle. As caravels became bigger, a third mast was added. For long ocean voyages, caravels were rigged with square sails set on shorter yards. This gave them more balanced sail power and made them easier to maneuver. The average length of a three-masted caravel was 75–80 feet.

The *Santa María* was Columbus' **flagship**.

A depiction of the Santa María

The vessel is believed to have been a three-masted ocean-going caravel that, at a length of 95 feet, was larger than average. She displaced 100 tons, had a **draft** of six feet, and carried a crew of 40. The ship had a total of five sails. In addition to two main sails, she was lateen-rigged on her **mizzen** mast, and had a small main-topsail and a **spritsail**.

The *Niña* is believed to have been a 90-ton, 60–75-foot-long caravel. Her captain was Vicente Yáñez Pinzón. When she left Spain she was a three-masted, lateen-rigged ship. Because lateen-rigged vessels did not handle well on the ocean, the *Niña* was converted to square rigging when she reached the Canary Islands.

The *Pinta* is believed to have been a 50-ton, 60–75-foot-long, square-rigged caravel. Her captain was Martín Alonso Pinzón, brother of the *Niña's* captain. The Pinzón family was one of the leading merchant-ship owners of Palos, Spain.

On August 3, 1492, the *Santa María*, *Niña* and *Pinta* set sail from Palos. Columbus was looking for a sea route to Asia but found the New World instead, making landfall on October 12, 1492, in what is today the Bahamas.

A total of 90 men went on the voyage. The expedition cost about $14,000, most of which was paid by the Spanish crown. The *Niña* and the *Pinta* were provided by the port of Palos. Columbus chartered the *Santa María* from her owner, Juan de la Cosa.

The *Santa María* was destroyed on Christmas Eve 1492, when she hit a coral reef in Caracol Bay, Haiti. Forty-four members of Columbus' expedition stayed behind to start the first colony in the New World. Columbus returned home in the *Niña*.

Vasco da Gama (1460–1524) was a Portuguese sailor and navigator who discovered the sea route from Europe to Asia around the Cape of Good Hope at the southern tip of Africa. Finding this route to Asia helped establish Portugal as a world power, and brought forth a new period of exploration and trade.

Da Gama's **flagship** was the *San Gabriel*, a 120-ton three-masted **caravel**. On July 9, 1497, the *San Gabriel* left Lisbon, Portugal, accompanied by three other vessels: the *San Rafael* (another 120-ton three-masted caravel), the *Berrio* (a 50-ton caravel) and an old, slow 200-ton supply ship. The *Berrio* was lateen-rigged, while all the other vessels were square-rigged. The caravels had been built expressly for this expedition, and were stronger than the typical caravels of their day.

The ships' combined crews comprised about 150 men (some reports claim 170). Because this was an expedition of discovery, the ships carried *padrões*, stone pillars that would be used to mark new territory and claim it for Portugal.

The *San Gabriel* reached Santa Helena Bay, in what is today South Africa, on November 7, 1497; it rounded the Cape of Good Hope two weeks later, and anchored in Mossel Bay, on the eastern coast of South Africa, three days later. After erecting a *padrão* on an island, da Gama ordered the supply ship to be broken up. He used its provisions to resupply his remaining three ships and sailed on, making faster progress without the older vessel. Traveling in the Indian Ocean, they reached Mozambique in early March 1498, and arrived in Mombasa and Malindi, both in modern Kenya, in April.

Turning east, they crossed the Indian

A caravel ship

Ocean in 23 days and reached Calicut, on western India's Malibar coast, on May 20. Calicut was a major port where pearls, precious stones, and spices were traded. It was the most important commercial center of southern India.

On their return journey, the ships encountered unfavorable winds. It took them three months to navigate the Indian Ocean. During this difficult crossing, many crewmembers died of **scurvy**. When they finally reached Malindi, da Gama ordered the burning of the *San Rafael* because he had too few crewmembers left to sail her.

Both the *San Gabriel* and the *Berrio* rounded the Cape of Good Hope on March 20, 1499. However, one month later they ran into a storm and were separated. The *Berrio* returned to Portugal on July 10, and the *San Gabriel* returned to Lisbon in September 1499. The journey had taken slightly more than two years. Only 44 men survived. Vasco da Gama had discovered the sea route to India, and the *San Gabriel* made history as the first European vessel to land in South Africa.

5. Henry Grâce à Dieu (Great Harry)
1514

The Great Harry

Henry Grâce à Dieu, or as she was also called, *Great Harry*, was the largest warship of her time. Created by order of King Henry VIII, she was built by the master shipwright William Bond and launched in June 1514, at Erith, in Kent, England. The founding of the Royal Navy and the creation of *Henry Grâce à Dieu* were Henry VIII's main contributions to making England a naval power.

Henry Grâce à Dieu was a carrack. Carracks were large vessels used for trade in the 14th–17th centuries. They were a combination of the square-rigged ships of northern Europe and the **lateen**-rigged ships of the Mediterranean, and had high castles set in the front and rear of the ship. Although similar to the three-masted **caravel**, carracks were bigger and better able to endure rough seas. The carrack inspired the larger three-masted vessels that were the common sailing ship design until the mid-19th century, when steam propulsion became popular.

Henry Grâce à Dieu weighed around 1,000 tons (records of the time describe her as weighing as much as 1,500 tons). She contained eight decks and four masts. Three of her masts had two circular tops, and her fore and main mast carried three square sails. Her two other masts, the **mizzen** and **bonaventure mizzen** carried lateen sails.

Great Harry carried a crew of anywhere from 700 to 900 men and was armed with 21 heavy bronze cannons. This was an unusually large number of guns for the time, and represented a change in naval warfare strategy. Earlier tactics called for winning a sea battle by boarding an enemy ship. However, as more powerful cannons were developed, captains tried to win battles by sinking enemy ships with gunfire. *Great Harry's* forbidding guns were so impressive, it was said that no " . . . fortress, however strong, could resist their fire."

In addition to her cannons, the vessel carried 230 lighter weapons that were mostly murderers. A murderer was a hand-held gun fitted with an iron pin on the bottom of the handle. The pin could be inserted into sockets placed around the ship so that the guns could be mounted where they were needed. Used to defend a ship against boarders, murderers were loaded with a ball and small pieces of jagged metal.

Henry Grâce à Dieu was a handsome ship, and in her day she was regarded as one of the wonders of the world. Henry VIII made her his **flagship**, and entertained foreign monarchs, as well as his own court, aboard her. On state occasions her sails were decorated with elaborate gold patterns.

She was rebuilt in 1540, but was destroyed in an accidental fire at Woolwich, a city east of London, in August 1553.

Ferdinand Magellan (c. 1480–1521) was a Portuguese navigator and explorer. In 1519 he sailed in the name of Spain's King Charles V on an expedition to reach the Spice Islands, by going around the New World and across the Great South Sea. (These islands are known today as the Moluccas Islands in eastern Indonesia.)

Magellan's expedition consisted of five **caravels**. His **flagship** was the *Trinidad*, which was considered to be the best ship of the five. The others were the *Victoria*, the *San Antonio*, the *Concepción*, and the *Santiago*.

Neither Magellan nor the *Victoria* were highly regarded at the Spanish court. Even Charles V, Magellan's patron, said, "I do not count him for much, for he is half crazy." The Portuguese ambassador described the *Victoria* as one of five "very old and patched ships." However, Magellan and his ship would prove their critics wrong.

Magellan's ships left Seville, Spain on September 20, 1519. More than a year later, on October 21, 1520, Magellan discovered the twisting 320-mile strait below South America that led him from the Atlantic to the Pacific Ocean. Today this is called the Strait of Magellan. By this time, the *Santiago* had been wrecked and the fleet was down to four vessels.

It took 38 days to navigate the strait. This journey was difficult and the captain of the *San Antonio* decided to return to Spain.

Finally, the three remaining vessels reached the ocean on the other side. The weather here was gentle and the ocean was calmer than the strait had been. Magellan named this huge expanse of water the Pacific Ocean.

The dwindling fleet continued, reaching the Philippines on March 9, 1521. Magellan and many of his men were killed in a battle on the island of Mactan on April 27. One of the expedition's navigators, Juan Sebastian del Cano, assumed command. Del Cano abandoned the *Concepción* because it had been damaged by shipworms, and the survivors escaped in the *Trinidad* and *Victoria*.

By this time, the *Trinidad* was undermanned and leaking; when she reached Borneo, the crew had no choice but to leave her there. The *Victoria* continued on, enduring a voyage that got worse and worse. By the time she made her way around the Cape of Good Hope, at the tip of South America, her crew was suffering from **scurvy** and starvation. When she reached the Cape Verde Islands off the western coast of Africa, 13 of the crew were captured by the Portuguese.

With del Cano still in command, the *Victoria* returned to Seville in July 1522. Of the 270 men who had set out when the five ships left Spain, only 18 returned. The *Victoria* may have been "very old and patched," but she became the first ship to circumnavigate the world.

Magellan's ships reaching Mactan Island

7. La Dauphine
1523

Giovanni da Verrazano (1485–1528) was an Italian navigator who sailed for France. In 1523 he secured the backing of the King of France, François I, to explore the New World in an effort to find a new passage to the Pacific Ocean. To make the voyage, the king gave him use of *La Dauphine*.

La Dauphine was a 100-ton **caravel**, built in 1519 at the new royal dockyard in Le Havre, and sent into service with the royal French navy. Because Verrazano was sailing for the King of France, it is very likely the ship flew the **royal ensign**, which consisted of gold fleurs-de-lys on a field of light blue.

La Dauphine carried a crew of 50 and was considered a small ship. While Verrazano was the leader of the expedition, the ship's captain was Antoine de Conflans. Also along on the voyage was Verrazano's brother, Girolamo, who had been assigned the job of drawing maps of any lands the expedition discovered.

When they set out again, they captured several vessels off the coast and Spain; it is believed that *La Normande* turned around to escort these prizes back to France.

La Dauphine sailed on alone, enjoying smooth seas for the next 25 days. Then she ran into a 16-hour storm that Verrazano called "as violent a hurricane as any ship ever weathered." However, the little ship rode out the storm, and in early March arrived in the New World, in the area of present-day Cape Fear, North Carolina. She then sailed north, up to what is today Kitty Hawk. Continuing north, *La Dauphine* found her way into New York Harbor, and Verrazano became the first known European to anchor in the narrows between Staten Island and Brooklyn. Today these waters are spanned by the Verrazano Bridge.

La Dauphine continued her explorations, going as far north as Newfoundland, Canada, before returning home. She reached Dieppe, France, in July 1524. The modest but extremely seaworthy ship had traveled a total of 3,816 nautical miles.

Verrazano was one of the first explorers to understand that America was not part of Asia, but an entirely new continent. Today, the original map Girolamo da Verrazano created on

La Dauphine in Newport harbor

When she left Dieppe, France, *La Dauphine* was accompanied by a merchant ship, *La Normande*, and two other vessels. After the four boats encountered a storm, only *La Dauphine* and *La Normande* survived. They put into a French port for repairs.

La Dauphine's voyage is on display at the National Maritime Museum, in Greenwich, London. Modern copies can also be seen at the Vatican Library in Rome and the Hispanic Society's Library in New York City.

Sir Francis Drake (c. 1543–1596) was the first Englishman to circumnavigate the world. His voyage helped make England an increasingly dominant sea power. When Drake set out from Plymouth, England, on December 13, 1577, he commanded about 160 men and a total of five ships. His **flagship** would go down in history as the *Golden Hind*, but at the start of the voyage she was called the *Pelican*.

Launched in 1560, the *Pelican* was a 100-ton vessel believed to be 90 feet long and 19 feet across the **beam**. She was a small, fast, three-masted ship with a **poop deck** and forecastle raised far above her main deck. Her **fore** and main masts carried square sails, she flew a **lateen** sail on her **mizzen** mast, and she carried 18 guns.

As Drake began his voyage through the Strait of Magellan in September 1578, he changed the ship's name from the *Pelican* to the *Golden Hind* to honor his patron, Sir Christopher Hatton, whose crest was a gold hind, or deer.

Drake was under secret orders from Queen Elizabeth to plunder Spanish ships and settlements; his voyage was marked by intrigue, betrayal, attempted mutiny, and desertion. By the time the *Golden Hind* sailed through the Strait of Magellan and into the Pacific, three of the companion ships had deserted. When the *Golden Hind* became separated from the remaining boat, the *Elizabeth*, her captain turned around and went home.

The *Golden Hind* continued, sailed around the world, and returned to Plymouth on September 26, 1580. By this time she carried half-a-million pounds in treasure that had been plundered from Spanish ships. Spain accused Drake of piracy, but the English

crown rewarded him. On April 4, 1581, Queen Elizabeth knighted Drake on the *Golden Hind's* quarterdeck.

The *Golden Hind* was permanently berthed

The Golden Hind

at Deptford, a London dockyard on the Thames River. People were allowed to tour the ship for a small fee, which was donated to charity. Over the years she was repaired and maintained, and she lasted into the next century. What finally happened to her is not known; it's believed that she ultimately could no longer be repaired and was dismantled.

The only known surviving wood from the *Golden Hind* is now a chair at the Bodleian Library in Oxford, and a table at the Middle Temple Hall in London.

During the late 1970s, a ship named the *Golden Hind* was placed on display in San Francisco, California. This was not Drake's ship, but an accurate reproduction of the type of ships that sailed during the Elizabethan period. This second *Golden Hind* sailed from Greenwich, England, to San Francisco in 1977.

Revenge is one of the most famous names in the history of the English Navy. Over the years this name has been given to a total of ten British ships. The most famous *Revenge* was the first.

When the Spanish Armada sailed against England in 1588, Sir Francis Drake was made vice admiral of the British fleet. Given his choice of flagships, he chose the galleon *Revenge*, which he considered to be the perfect war vessel.

A galleon is an English variation of the carrack that eliminated the high forecastle of the large ships built at this time. The *Revenge* was a 500-ton galleon, 92 feet long and 32 feet across the **beam**. Launched at Deptford in 1577, she mounted 34 guns and carried a crew of 150 men.

One of the fastest ships in the fleet, under Drake's command the *Revenge* played a major role in the running battle to repel the Armada. The engagement lasted ten days and was a decisive victory for the English. One hundred thirty ships left Spain in what the Spanish called an "invincible" fleet. Only 67 returned.

In 1590, under the command of Sir Martin Frobisher, the *Revenge* saw duty off the coast of Spain as part of a squadron sent to intercept Spanish ships carrying treasure from the Indies.

The *Revenge* fought her last battle on August 31, 1591. By then the **flagship** of Sir Richard Grenville, she was part of a fleet sent to the Azores to attack a fleet of Spanish treasure ships. While waiting for the Spanish ships, the English seamen became ill and Grenville sent more than half the vessel's 250-man crew ashore. The British were unaware that a large Spanish escort had been sent to guard the treasure ships. By the time the English became aware of the approaching Spaniards, they had become too weak to fight, and had no choice but to retreat.

Since she had the most men ashore, the *Revenge* was the last English ship to embark and was separated from the rest of the fleet. With only 190 men, surrounded by the Spanish fleet, and facing 15 enemy ships manned by 5,000 men, the *Revenge* fought a 15-hour engagement that was later celebrated in Alfred Lord Tennyson's poem *"The Last Fight of the Revenge."* The *Revenge* sank one enemy ship and heavily damaged another. When she could no longer fight, Grenville ordered her sunk. Her officers objected and negotiated terms of surrender that allowed the ship's crew to live.

Wounded three times during the battle, Grenville was taken aboard the Spanish admiral's ship. He died three days later. Five days after the battle, as the *Revenge* was being taken to Spain as a prize of war, she went down in a storm, taking 200 Spanish seamen with her.

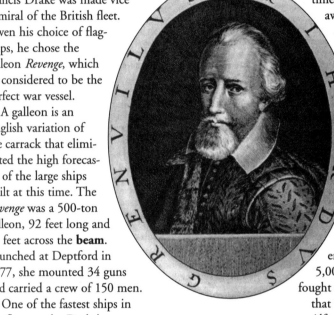

Sir Richard Grenville

10. Half Moon
1609

Henry Hudson (1565–1611) was an English navigator and explorer whose voyages included two unsuccessful attempts to find a sea route to China via the northeast passage—a route around the north of Europe and through the ice-blocked seas to the far north.

In 1609 Hudson was hired by the Dutch East India Company to undertake a third voyage to find a northeast or northwest route to China. It was a voyage beset with difficulties. Because of tension and distrust between Hudson and his sponsors, they decided to give him an old ship.

The *Half Moon* (*Halve Maen* in Dutch) was a 60-ton vessel with a shallow **draught** and a high **poop deck** and **forecastle**. She

The Half Moon navigating the Hudson River

was cramped, clumsy, and rode high in the water. A Dutch navigator, who was a friend of Hudson's, predicted that "she will prove difficult to handle in foul weather."The *Half*

Moon carried a crew of 20 Dutch and English sailors. For the most part they did not speak each other's language, and Hudson did not speak Dutch.

Hudson set out in early April 1609. In the middle of May, the *Half Moon* encountered rough weather and ice off the coast of Norway. Adding to Hudson's difficulties, the Dutch crewmen were not used to sailing in cold waters. Making matters worse, the Dutch and English crewmen were fighting with each other. Facing a possible mutiny, Hudson persuaded his angry crew to sail west across the Atlantic Ocean toward warmer water and North America.

However, bad weather followed the ship. During one storm, her foremast was swept overboard and her deck was damaged. On July 8 the *Half Moon* reached Newfoundland, in North America, and sailed south. By August 28, she had gone as far as Virginia and turned north. On September 3, she reached New York Harbor and navigated 150 miles up what is today the Hudson River. The trip demonstrated that this body of water was indeed a river, not a strait that would lead to the Pacific Ocean and eventually to China.

The *Half Moon* returned to England, anchoring at Dartmouth on November 7, 1609. English authorities were unhappy with Hudson's contribution to Dutch efforts to explore the New World. He and his English crewmen were not permitted to go on to Holland, and Hudson was ordered not to serve the Dutch again. The *Half Moon* returned to Holland under the Dutch sailors in her crew.

The Mayflower at sea

One of the most famous ships in history, the *Mayflower* will always be remembered as the boat that brought the Pilgrims to the New World to establish the first permanent European settlement in New England.

No plans or drawings of the *Mayflower* exist. She is believed to have been a 180-ton vessel that was 90 feet long. Evidence suggests that she had a high stern, three masts, a **bowsprit**, **spritsail**, **poop deck**, and **forecastle**.

Naval records list a voyage to Norway in 1609, on which the *Mayflower* returned to England with a cargo of tar and pickled herrings. On her last known voyage before being chartered by the Pilgrims, she carried wine from France to England.

As a merchant ship, the *Mayflower* probably contained mounted guns. It is believed that after being chartered by the Pilgrims she underwent a major refitting that included building new interior walls to create passenger cabins and closing her gunports to increase cargo space.

On August 15, 1620, the *Mayflower* set out from Southampton, England. Her captain was Christopher Jones, and she carried about 100 Pilgrims seeking religious freedom in the New World. The *Mayflower* was accompanied by another vessel, the *Speedwell*, which carried a group of Pilgrims from Holland. However, the *Speedwell* proved unseaworthy, and the ships stopped at Plymouth, England, for repairs. From there, the *Mayflower* departed alone, on September 6, 1620, with some of the *Speedwell's* passengers aboard.

The *Mayflower's* destination was Virginia Colony, where land had been granted to the Pilgrims. However, storms sent the ship off course: instead of Virginia, she reached what is today Provincetown, on Cape Cod, in Massachusetts, on November 11, 1620. That day, the passengers signed the **Mayflower Compact** aboard the ship. The compact was a document the Pilgrims drew up that provided a legal basis for governing themselves and the area in which they settled. Forty-one of the *Mayflower's* male passengers signed the agreement.

A small group led by William Bradford was chosen to go ahead of the others and find a place for a settlement. On December 21, this small party reached what is today Plymouth, Massachusetts. Five days later, everyone on the *Mayflower* went ashore at Plymouth.

In April 1621, the *Mayflower* returned to England, but nothing is known of her later history. In 1926, a detailed model of the *Mayflower* was built, based on the few facts known about the original ship. This model was used as a guide to help build the *Mayflower II*, which was constructed during the 1950s and which made a 53-day voyage across the Atlantic in 1957. The *Mayflower II* is not a replica of the original *Mayflower*, but a general representation of the ships of this period. She is currently on display at Pilgrims' Hall in Plymouth, Massachusetts.

12. Royal Sovereign
1637

Described as one of the most beautiful ships ever built, the English vessel *Royal Soverign* was the largest warship of her day.

The standard line of battle in which sailing ships fought did not exist until the First Anglo-Dutch War (1652–1654). Prior to that time, when ships fought in a group, each vessel sailed into battle seeking one other boat to engage in single combat. At the Battle of Portland (1653), British ships attempted to fight in formation for the first time. This strategy was perfected during the Second Anglo-Dutch War (1665–1667). Because a ship's guns could only be fired at right angles from the sides of the boat, vessels sailed one behind the other when in the line, with their sides toward the enemy. Otherwise, they risked firing on one of the ships in their own group.

To be part of the line of battle, a vessel had to have sufficient firepower. At the beginning of the 17th century, warships were rated by the number of guns they carried. The British Navy specified six rates: first rate: 100 guns or more; second rate : 84–100 guns; third rate : 70–84 guns; fourth rate : 50–70 guns; fifth rate: 32–50 guns; sixth rate: fewer thain 32 guns. Ships of the first three rates were deemed to have adequate weaponry to be in the line of battle and were called **ships of the line**.

The first three-decker of 100 guns, the *Royal Sovereign* was the prototype of a first-rate ship of the line. An elegant three-masted vessel, she was built at Woolwich by the master shipbuilders Peter and Phineas Pett. At 1,500 tons she was launched in October 1637, and originally named *Sovereign of the Seas*. In 1649 there was talk of changing her name to *Commonwealth*, but instead her name was shortened to *Sovereign*.

As the *Sovereign*, she saw action in the First

The Royal Sovereign

Anglo-Dutch War, helping to win a major victory over the Dutch at the Battle of Kentish Knock (1652). In 1660 she was rebuilt and renamed *Royal Sovereign*.

As the *Royal Sovereign*, she saw action in the Second Anglo-Dutch War. In the Third Anglo-Dutch War (1672–1674), she was the **flagship** of Prince Rupert, admiral of the fleet. Rebuilt a second time in 1684, she continued to see combat and was the flagship of two more admirals.

The *Royal Sovereign's* illustrious career came to an end at Chatham, England, in January 1696, when she was destroyed after being accidentally set ablaze.

19

13. Adventure Galley
1696

The Charles Galley, a vessel similar to the Adventure Galley

Pirates, buccaneers, and privateers were free-roaming bandits who sought adventure and riches—and brought danger and destruction to the ships they attacked. Pirates attacked anyone, including each other. Buccaneers, who got their name from roasting their meat in *boucans*, or barbecues, attacked all ships except those from their own country. Privateers carried *letters of marque* granted by government authority, which identified their holders as agents of a government and allowed them to take ships of hostile nations. Letters of marque also freed privateers from charges of piracy.

One of the most famous pirates was William Kidd (c.1645–1701), who ranged from the West Indies to the Indian Ocean. Ironically, during his lifetime he was, at the same time, known as both a notorious pirate and an officer of the law appointed to stop piracy!

Kidd's ship was the *Adventure Galley*. Part of its name came from the type of ship it was. Galleys were oared ships used primarily for war. They originated in the Mediterranean around 3000 B.C. At first the oars were on one level, but later galleys carried oars on different levels. *Biremes* had two banks of oars, *triremes* had three levels, and there are records of galleys with as many as five levels of oars. The principle weapon of the early galley was the **ram**, a strengthened projection mounted at the bow of a ship and used to disable or sink another boat by deliberately crashing into it.

Galleys of the 16th and 17th centuries carried guns mounted on a platform in the bow of the ship. Early galleys had one or two square-rigged masts and were best suited for calm waters. Later galleys carried **lateen** sails. The sails and masts were lowered for battle; when fighting, the ship used its oars to maneuver. Galleys were last used in warfare in the Mediterranean in 1717, and in the Baltic Sea as late as 1809.

In 1695 Kidd was given a royal commission to pursue pirates who were attacking the vessels of the English East India Company. He set sail from Deptford on February 27, 1696, in the *Adventure Galley*, a brand new 34-gun ship. Accounts of his famous voyage vary, but by the time it was over Kidd had acquired his reputation as a pirate, killed one of his own men, and supposedly left behind buried treasure, tales of which persist to this day.

The legendary Kidd's biggest prize was the *Quedagh Merchant*, which carried a rich cargo of gold, jewels, silk, sugar, and guns. Though Kidd claimed to have captured the ship as a privateer, he was accused of piracy and taken to London. After a trial marked by controversy and intrigue, Kidd was found guilty of piracy and was hanged on May 23, 1701.

14. St. Peter
1740

The *St. Peter* was an 18th-century Russian vessel used by the Danish explorer Vitus Bering (1681–1741) to explore the southwest coast of what is today Alaska, the Alaskan peninsula, and the Aleutian Islands.

Years before he sailed on the *St. Peter*, Bering had made other important explorations and discoveries. While serving with the Russian Navy, in 1725 Czar Peter the Great gave Bering the mission of exploring the northeast coast of Asia to learn if any land connection existed between Asia and North America.

On July 13, 1728, Bering set sail from the Siberian peninsula Kamchatka. He explored the sea that lies between Asia and North America, and discovered the narrow body of water that separates Siberia and Alaska. Today these bodies of water—named in his honor—are called respectively the Bering Sea and the Bering Strait. In August he navigated the Bering Strait and passed into the Arctic Ocean. Because of bad weather, Bering could not see North America, so he did not realize how close he was to the North American coast. Nevertheless, he concluded that Asia and North America are not connected.

In 1730, the Empress Anna sent Bering on another exploratory voyage. In the course of this mission, he founded the town of Okhotsk on Russia's Pacific coast, and established the port of Petropavlovsk on the Kamchatka peninsula.

The *St. Peter* was built in Okhotsk and launched in June 1740. A 108-ton two-masted ship rigged as a brig, she was 80 feet long, 22 feet wide, and had a **draft** of 9 1/2 feet. She carried 76 men and was equipped with 14 two- and three-pound guns.

In 1741, after spending the winter on the Kamchatka peninsula, Bering set sail from Petropavlovsk in the *St. Peter*. With her was the *St. Paul*, an identical ship that had been built at the same time as the *St. Peter*. During the voyage, the ships lost each other in a storm and each continued alone. The *St. Paul* went on to discover several Aleutian Islands.

On August 20, 1741, the *St. Peter* sailed into the Gulf of Alaska. Bering sighted the St. Elias mountain range in Alaska, and reached Kayak Island. He might have continued his explorations, but his crew was suffering from **scurvy** and he was worried about getting his ship home safely.

Bering himself had become afflicted with scurvy, and so was not as capable a captain as he had been at the start of the voyage. In early November, the St. Peter was wrecked on one of the Commander Islands near Kamchatka. Some of the crew were able to return to Siberia, but Bering died. He was buried on this small island that is today called Bering Island.

The death of Vitus Bering

The *Bonhomme Richard* was a frigate commanded by the American privateer John Paul Jones. Common to all navies, frigates were three-masted ships fully rigged on each mast and armed with 24–38 guns that were mounted on a single gun deck. Smaller than

The Bonhomme Richard engages the Serapis in battle

full ships of war, they were more maneuverable and generally served as lookouts for fleets. During battles they were used to repeat an admiral's signals to the rest of the ships, which might not be able to see the signals due to smoke. Frigates sometimes served as escorts for convoys. They also sailed alone, searching for enemy ships or privateers. When they sailed alone, they were often called cruisers. In the days of sail, when entire fleets faced each other in battle, larger ships did not usually directly engage frigates unless the frigate fired first. This courtesy was in consideration of the frigate's smaller size. However, these manners did not apply if a frigate was encountered alone on the open sea.

The *Bonhomme Richard* was originally an East Indian ship named *Duc de Duras*. A three-masted ship built in 1766, she weighed about 900 tons, mounted 40 guns, and had a crew of 375. Bought for Jones by the French govern-

ment, she was refitted and her name was changed to the *Bonhomme Richard* in honor of Benjamin Franklin's Poor Richard character from his famous publication, *Poor Richard's Almanack*. The vessel was first used to escort French troop convoys; after this service, Jones sailed her to raid British ships.

In 1779 the *Bonhomme Richard* went on a devastating privateering voyage. On September 23, off Flamborough Head in northeast Britain, she encountered a convoy of English merchant ships escorted by the *Serapis* and the *Countess of Scarborough*. The merchant ships escaped, while the *Bonhomme Richard* engaged the *Serapis*, and the *Pallas*, a French frigate sailing with Jones, engaged the *Countess of Scarborough*. Historians have called the battle between the *Bonhomme Richard* and the *Serapis* "one of the fiercest naval conflicts of the century." For three hours the two ships battled nonstop, cannon to cannon, under a moonlit sky. It was during this ferocious engagement that Jones uttered the famous words, "I have not yet begun to fight!"

Finally, although only two of the *Bonhomme Richard*'s guns were still functioning, a fire raging on the *Serapis* forced her captain to surrender. Jones later said that there had never been a naval engagement "so bloody, so severe, and so lasting."

The *Bonhomme Richard*, which had also been set ablaze, lost 150 crewmen and was so damaged that Jones put his crew aboard the captured *Serapis*. Two days later, the *Bonhomme Richard* sank.

The *Resolution* earned its place in history as the ship on which Captain James Cook (1728–1779) sailed when he discovered the Sandwich Islands, (Hawaii today) on his third Pacific voyage.

Launched at Whitby, England, in 1770, the *Resolution* was a 562-ton, cat-built collier. Typically 300–400 tons, a collier was a ship built for carrying coal. A cat-built collier was able to carry 600 tons of coal and was a very strong vessel based on a Norwegian design for a simple, functional boat. When she was launched, the *Resolution* was called the Marquis of Granby. In December 1771, she was renamed *Resolution*.

Cook's second Pacific voyage began on July 13, 1772. This expedition is particularly notable because on board the *Resolution* was a copy of John Harrison's **chronometer**, which enabled seamen to get a fix on their position at sea. After this voyage, the chronometer became standard equipment on many ships.

On his second voyage, Cook also became the first navigator to cross the Antarctic circle. By accomplishing this, he demonstrated that, contrary to popular belief, there was no inhabitable continent in the far reaches of the South Pacific. The *Resolution* returned to Portsmouth, England, on July 29, 1775.

Cook's third voyage began when the *Resolution* left Plymouth on July 13, 1776, in the company of another ship, the *Discovery*, commanded by Charles Clerke. The *Resolution* had been poorly refitted and repaired, and the ship was now plagued by problems with her masts and spars. On January 18, 1778, the *Resolution* arrived at what is today Hawaii, which Cook called the Sandwich Islands in honor of the Earl of Sandwich.

Staying only long enough to reprovision his ships, Cook went north. He explored and surveyed the Alaskan coast, the Aleutian Islands, and the Bering Strait. Then he returned to the Sandwich Islands, and the *Resolution* dropped anchor in what is today Kealakekua Bay on January 17, 1779. Cook and his men were given a reception worthy of gods—in fact, the native people believed they were gods.

On February 4, Cook sailed away. However, two days later the *Resolution* suffered a damaged mast and had to return to the Sandwich Islands. Now relations between

The Resolution

the natives and Cook's men were not as friendly. The natives began to wonder if these strangers really were gods, and quarrels broke out. On February 14, during a confrontation between the Englishmen and the natives, Captain Cook was killed.

Now commanded by Clerke, the *Resolution* sailed far to the north to explore the Asiatic side of the Bering Sea. The ship encountered thick ice, and Clerke, who was sick with a lung disease, died that August. Under the command of Lieutenant Gore, both the *Resolution* and *Discovery* returned to England in October 1780.

The East India companies were huge merchant businesses established by European nations to develop trade with India, the East Indies, and the Far East. These businesses flourished during the 17th and 18th centuries. There were a total of eight East India companies in Europe, but the most important were the ones in England and Holland.

The English East India Company was established by royal charter of Elizabeth I on December 31, 1600. In 1609 it built its own dockyard at Deptford. The Dutch East India Company was established in 1602. These two companies were almost nations unto themselves At its peak, the Dutch East India Company had 150 trading ships, 40 warships, and 10,000 soldiers. The two companies competed so fiercely that there was a virtual state of war between them.

The ships they sent around the world were called East Indiamen. Bigger than the carrack, which they eventually replaced, these three-masted vessels averaged 300–500 tons, although toward the end of the 17th century they reached more than 800 tons. East Indiamen were the biggest and best merchant ships of their time.

East Indiamen were ornately designed and decorated with intricate wood carvings. The interiors of these stately ships were also elaborate —the captain, officers, and passengers traveled in comfort and luxury. In this regard, East Indiamen were early versions of the so-called "floating palaces" that would cross the Atlantic Ocean during the 20th century.

East Indiamen were equipped not only for commerce, but for battle as well. Once on the seas, they faced pirates and the armed ships of other East India companies. Many sailed with rows of cannons mounted on two decks, although one row was sometimes an array of false cannons to make the vessel look better armed and more intimidating to potential attackers.

The East Indiaman *Dartmouth* was built in 1773. In the fall of that year, the 79-foot-long ship left England under the command of Captain James Hall, carrying 114 crates of tea. She was bound for Boston, Massachusetts, and sailed with three other vessels also carrying tea—the *Eleanor, Beaver*, and *William*. The *William* was wrecked off Cape Cod, Massachusetts. The remaining three ships arrived in Boston on November 28.

The Boston Tea Party

Because the colonists in America were protesting import taxes on tea, the people of Boston would not let the ships' cargoes be unloaded. On the night of December 16, a band of 30–60 patriots disguised as Native Americans boarded the ships and threw the tea into Boston Harbor. Their act of defiance, which went down in history as the Boston Tea Party, roused the rebellious spirit of other colonists—a spirit that eventually led to the American War for Independence.

One of the most serious charges that can be leveled against a seaman is that of mutiny, and one of the most famous mutinies of all time took place aboard the English ship *Bounty* in 1789.

Built at Hull, England, in 1784, the *Bounty* was originally named the *Bethia*. She was a 220-ton merchant ship that was 85 feet long, 24 feet in the **beam**, and had a top speed of nine knots.

In 1787, the *Bethia* was purchased by the Royal Navy and refitted at Deptford to be an armed transport. On June 8, 1787, she was renamed *Bounty*. As part of the refitting, her new captain, William Bligh, had her masts shortened and ordered that the amount of iron in the ship be reduced to make her better able to withstand heavy storms on the open sea. Her new equipment included 4 four-pound cannons, and 10 swivel guns.

The *Bounty*'s mission was to transport breadfruit from Tahiti to the West Indies, where it was to be used as a source of inexpensive food for slaves. The vessel was a small ship for such a long voyage, but was regarded as "an excellent sea boat." Under the command of Bligh, who was a very strict disciplinarian, the *Bounty* left England for Tahiti on December 23, 1787. She carried a crew of 46.

On April 28, 1789, the *Bounty* was near Tofua, in the Tonga Islands, when Fletcher Christian, one of the ship's officers, led a mutiny against Capt. Bligh and seized control of the ship. Reasons for the mutiny are in dispute to this day. Some say that Bligh was unusually severe with his men, meting out extreme and unnecessary punishments. Some say that Christian and the mutineers simply wanted to live in the South Seas rather than return to England.

Eighteen men remained loyal to Bligh and, with him, were cast adrift in the *Bounty*'s launch. After a 48-day, 3,600-mile journey in the small open boat, Bligh and the others finally reached the island of Timor in the East Indies. Christian and his followers took the *Bounty* to Tahiti. Then he and 8 men, plus 18 Tahitians, sailed to Pitcairn Island, where they settled, and where their descendants can still be found. On January 23, 1790, the *Bounty* was beached and burned on Pitcairn Island.

Years later, the British Navy sent the frigate *Pandora* to Tahiti to seek out any remaining mutineers. Fourteen mutineers who remained in Tahiti were captured. Four of them later drowned when the *Pandora* went down on the Great Barrier Reef, off Australia. The remaining 10 mutineers were returned to England and put on trial. Three of them were hanged.

The Bounty

In 1794, when the young republic of the United States was establishing its navy, Congress authorized the construction of what came to be known as the "six original frigates." These six frigates were the *United States, Constitution, President, Chesapeake, Constellation* and *Congress.* The most famous of these vessels, and the boat that has been called the most famous ship in the U.S. Navy, is the *Constitution.*

Built in Boston, Massachusetts, she was launched on October 21, 1797, and first put to sea in 1798. Weighing 2,200 tons, the *Constitution* was 204 feet long and 43 feet, six inches across the **beam**. A three-masted ship with 42,710 square feet of sail, she had a speed of 14 knots. She mounted 44 guns and carried a crew of 450. Her copper fastenings were made by Paul Revere.

The *Constitution* fought naval engagements against the French, and was the **flagship** of Commodore Edward Preble in the war with Tripoli (1801–05) to stop the Barbary Pirates.

However, it was during the War of 1812 (1812–15) that the *Constitution* secured her place in history and earned her famous nickname, "Old Ironsides." The United States was terribly unprepared for the War of 1812. When Congress declared war against England on June 18, 1812, the U. S. Navy contained a total of 16 ships—eight frigates and eight smaller boats. American seamen faced the vastly superior British Navy, and U.S. morale was low.

Then, on August 19, 1812, in the first major naval engagement of the war, the *Constitution* engaged and defeated the British frigate *Guerrière.* The *Guerrière* carried 48 guns, but her cannon shot seemed to merely bounce off the *Constitution's* solid oak timbers as if they were made of iron.

On December 29, 1812, the *Constitution* captured and destroyed the British frigate *Java.* On February 20, 1813, she took part in a four-hour battle and captured two English ships, the 32-gun *Cyane* and the 20-gun *Levant.*

Years later after the war, the *Constitution* was declared unseaworthy and was scheduled to be dismantled. However, the poet Oliver Wendell Holmes rallied public support with his famous poem about her exploits, "Old Ironsides." Instead of being destroyed, the *Constitution* was restored to her original condition in 1833. She was restored again in 1877 and became a training ship. In 1897, she was berthed at the Boston Navy Yard.

After a 1925 act of Congress, she was restored once again, and made a tour of 90 American ports. Since 1934 she has been on permanent display in Boston, Massachusetts, where the public can tour her. "Old Ironsides" is the only surviving frigate of her day, and the oldest commissioned warship still afloat.

The Constitution

Over the years, a total of five British ships have borne the name *Victory*. The most famous was the last. The **flagship** of Vice Admiral Horatio Nelson (1758–1805) at the Battle of Trafalgar, it has been called the most famous warship in England's Royal Navy.

Built at Chatham, the *Victory* was designed by Sir Thomas Slade, the most famous warship planner of the time. Construction began in 1759, but was halted at the end of the Seven Years War (1756–63). The *Victory* was launched on May 7, 1765, but work on her was not completed, so she wasn't ready to take to the open sea. While she stood idle in the water, the wood in her frames seasoned. The *Victory* was completed in 1778, and when she finally entered service her timbers were especially strong.

She was the largest warship of her time—a three-deck, three-masted, first rate **ship of the line** weighing 2,162 tons and carrying 100 guns. In July, 1778, she served as a flagship at the second Battle of Ushant, during the War of American Independence (1775–83), and again in the war between England and France during the French Revolutionary period (1793-1799).

The Victory was Admiral Nelson's flagship from 1803–1805, during the Napoleonic Wars (1800–1815). Her most famous engagement was the Battle of Trafalgar, which took place October 21, 1805, off Cape Trafalgar on the southwest coast of Spain. England faced the combined fleets of France and Spain, and Napoleon hoped this huge force would give him control of the English Channel. When the two fleets met, Nelson surprised the French—and his own captains—with an unconventional two-column attack. Instead of

The Victory

having his ships sail in the traditional line of battle, he split his fleet in to two columns. The *Victory* broke through the French line, and in an intense four-hour battle the 33-ship French-Spanish fleet lost 20 vessels.

During the fight, the French ship *Redoubtable* engaged with the *Victory*. Nelson was on the *Victory's* quarter-deck, and was shot. He died a few hours later, but according to the *Victory's* log lived long enough to hear that the British fleet had won the engagement.

The *Victory* lost two masts and her wheel was shot away. She was repaired at Gibraltar, then carried Nelson's body back to England for a state funeral. Trafalgar has been called "the most complete sea victory of its era."

The *Victory* remained in service until 1835, when she was taken to Portsmouth, permanently berthed, and designated the permanent flagship of the commander-in-chief of Portsmouth. Unfortunately, she was not properly maintained, and slowly deteriorated. In 1922, the *Victory* was completely restored to her condition at Trafalgar, and opened to the public as a memorial.

Fulton's first steamship

copper boiler that provided steam was toward the rear, encased in brick. The *Clermont* used wood and coal for fuel.

There was so much skepticism about Fulton's project that it became known as "Fulton's Folly" and he had to promise many of his investors that he would not make their names public.

The *Clermont's* maiden voyage took place on August 17, 1807, when she was launched from Paulus Hook, near New York City. The boat's furnace belched dark smoke that stained the clothes of the nearly 40 passengers, and the very sight of this strange, noisy contraption terrified many local farmers. However, the *Clermont* triumphed as she chugged up the Hudson River to Albany and back at an average speed of five knots, covering a distance of about 240 miles in 62 hours. The sailing ships of the time required as much 96 hours to make the same trip.

The *Clermont* began regular passenger service to Albany that September. She was eventually enhanced—in her final version she had 100 feet of usable deck, three large cabins that contained 54 passenger berths, and facilities for providing meals.

Clermont was never the official name of Fulton's vessel. When launched, she was called only "The Steamboat." After rebuilding his boat in 1807–1808, Fulton called her *The North River Steamboat of Clermont.* (Clermont was the name of the estate of Fulton's financial partner.) However, eventually it was the name *Clermont* that stuck.

Never meant to be a sea-going vessel, the *Clermont's* days as a riverboat ended in 1814.

In 1802 the *Charlotte Dundas* became the world's first commercial steam vessel. However, she operated only briefly on Scotland's Forth and Clyde canal, and had to end service because it was feared the banks of the canal would collapse.

It was the *Clermont,* designed by Robert Fulton (1765–1815), that became the first successful steamship to be put into full service. Fulton was an American, but no American engineers had the expertise to build a steam engine capable of powering a vessel. So the *Clermont's* engine was built in Birmingham, England, by Boulton and Watt. This 20-horsepower engine consisted of a single vertical cylinder that measured 24 inches in diameter and was approximately 48 inches deep. The engine drove a pair of paddle-wheels that were 15 feet in diameter and mounted on either side of the *Clermont's* hull. Fulton designed the ship's transmission, basing it on the design of William Symington, who had built the *Charlotte Dundas.*

A flat-bottomed, wooden boat with a wedge-shaped **bow** and **stern**, the *Clermont* displaced 100 tons; she was 133 feet long and 18 feet in the **beam**. Her engine was mounted toward the front of the ship, and the 20-foot

During the War of 1812, both the Americans and the British built fleets on Lake Erie. The purpose of the English fleet was to invade the United States; the purpose of the American fleet was to stop this invasion.

manding the *Lawrence*, the two fleets engaged. The British ships carried long guns, while the American ships were armed with **carronades**. Because its carronades did not have long range, the *Lawrence* endured almost

Perry moving to the Niagara during the Battle of Lake Erie

The ships of both forces were constructed from wood cut in the nearby forests. Equipping the ships was a difficult process that entailed hauling supplies over rough wilderness roads.

By August 1813, the Americans had built the Lawrence and the Niagara, both 500-ton **brigs**. Used mostly for coastal trading and short voyages, they were well-suited for service on Lake Erie. In addition to the two brigs, the American fleet consisted of several smaller craft: schooners, with **fore**-and-**aft** sails on two or more masts, and single-masted vessels, called sloops. Captain Oliver Hazard Perry (1785–1819) was in command of the American fleet.

The commander of the British fleet, Robert Barclay, had four small craft and two sloops, the *H.M.S. Detroit* and *Queen Charlotte*, which matched Perry's brigs in firepower. The small ships in both fleets did not have much speed in the light lake winds, so the Battle of Lake Erie was fought primarily between the four larger ships.

On September 10, 1813, with Perry com-

30 minutes of fire from the British ships while Perry waited to get close enough to shoot back. The *Niagara*, commanded by Jesse D. Elliott, remained outside the battle because Elliott decided not to **close** with the British ships. This meant the *Lawrence* took all the fire from the *Detroit, Queen Charlotte,* and a British schooner.

After about two hours of exchanging fire, the English ships were heavily damaged, and the *Lawrence* was devastated. She was unable to maneuver, she had no functioning guns, and her deck was littered with her wounded and dead. Perry made his way to the *Niagara* by rowboat, took command of the ship, and ordered Elliott to bring up the smaller American ships. Then the *Niagara* reengaged the English fleet, fighting with such fury that Barclay finally surrendered.

The Battle of Lake Erie lasted four hours and made Perry a hero. It was after this battle that he sent the famous message, "We have met the enemy and they are ours." Today, a replica of the *Niagara* is on display in Erie, Pennsylvania.

The first steamship to cross the Atlantic was the *Savannah*. However, this crossing was made mostly by sail and did not usher in the age of steam.

Built in New York by Francis Fickett, the *Savannah* was a 380-ton, three-masted, square-rigged sailing vessel. She was 98 feet, 6 inches long and 25 feet, 9 inches across the **beam**, with a top speed of 6 knots. Before she was completed, she was refitted to carry a small, 90-horsepower steam engine that drove two detachable paddle-wheels. When the *Savannah* was under sail, the paddle-wheels were removed and placed on the deck. Her engine and boilers took up a great deal of the **hold**, so there wasn't much room to carry cargo. Accommodations for passengers included two well-appointed state rooms and 32 berths.

It didn't really matter how much cargo or passengers the *Savannah* could carry, however, because the public didn't trust steam. People called the *Savannah* "The Steam Coffin." Passengers refused to book passage and merchants refused to ship cargo. Even her captain didn't know exactly how much coal his ship would need to cross the Atlantic Ocean. It would later be determined that the *Savannah* simply wasn't big enough to carry enough coal to make the trip entirely under steam power.

On May 24, 1819, the *Savannah* left Savannah, Georgia, for Liverpool, England. She arrived on June 20, but she was powered by steam for only 85 hours of the 27-day journey. As she approached the coast of Ireland with thick black smoke billowing out of her stack, lookouts thought they saw a ship in flames and sent a boat out to assist her.

The *Savannah*'s owners hoped she would become famous as the first steamship to cross the Atlantic. In Europe, there were rumors that she'd been built to rescue Napoleon, who was in exile on the island of St. Helena. However, the *Savannah* gained more attention as a thing of wonder and mystery than as a practical ship. From England she went to Russia, but failed to impress the imperial court. She returned home powered the "old-fashioned way"—by wind.

Back in the United States, her engines were removed. The *Savannah* finished her short career carrying mail, in her original form as a sailing vessel. In 1821 she was wrecked when she ran aground off Long Island, New York, during a storm.

The *Savannah*'s steam crossing could hardly be called a success, and her claim to be the first steamship to cross the Atlantic is not universally recognized. However, she did signal a change. It would not be a reality until almost two decades later—but the age of steam-powered travel was on the horizon.

The Savannah

24. Beagle
1820

Several ships have been named the *Beagle*, but the best-known is the ship that carried Charles Darwin (1809–1882) on the voyage that led him to develop the theory of evolution.

The *Beagle* was built at Woolwich, England in 1820. She was a 235-ton **sloop** that measured about 90 feet long and 30 feet wide. Assigned to surveying duties in 1825, she spent five years surveying the Strait of Magellan under the captainship of Philip King. In 1829 she came under the command of Robert Fitzroy, who was also sent on a mission to survey the Strait of Magellan.

Fitzroy was her captain again when the *Beagle* sailed with orders to survey South America's southern coasts, stop at various Pacific islands, and set up a chain of chronometric stations that would be used to help ships determine their position at sea. On this mission she carried 22 **chronometers** packed in sawdust, and among her 74 passengers was a young naturalist named Charles Darwin.

Charles Robert Darwin was only 22 years old when he volunteered to be the expedition's official naturalist. He later described it as "by far the most important event of my life."

In preparation for the voyage on which Darwin sailed, the *Beagle* was refitted to have three masts; lightning rods were added to her masts, and she was armed with seven bass cannons.

Upon seeing the *Beagle* for the first time, Darwin was impressed. He wrote, "no vessel has been fitted out so expensively and with so much care. . . and nothing can exceed the neatness and beauty of all the accommodations." However, he would later change his mind. His quarters had so little sleeping space that he had to remove a drawer from a locker to make room for his feet.

The *Beagle* set sail from Devonport, England, on December 27, 1831, on what was to become a five-year voyage that took

Charles Darwin

her to New Zealand, Australia, Tahiti, the Cape of Good Hope, Brazil, and the Galapagos Islands.

It was the Galapagos Islands, a group of islands in the Pacific Ocean about 200 miles off the coast of Ecuador, that became most closely linked with Darwin's work. Here, he was able to study plants and animals in their native environment as they existed for thousands of years. His observations and conclusions led him to develop his theory of evolution. In 1839 Darwin published an account of the expedition in *Journal of Researches into the Natural History and Geology of the Countries visited during the Voyage of H.M.S. 'Beagle'.*

In later years, the *Beagle* was used to explore and survey Australian waters.

31

25. Seringapatam
1837

Established by royal charter on December 31, 1600, the English East India Company maintained a monopoly on trade with India until 1813 and had a monopoly on trade with China until 1833. But when the monopolies ended, trade with Asia was open to all; from 1837 to 1869 a type of vessel that came to be called the Blackwall Frigate was built to engage in this lucrative commerce.

Many of these boats were built at a ship-

The Anglesey (above) is an example of a Blackwell Frigate

yard owned by Green and Wigram, located at Blackwall, on the Thames River. Like frigates, they were three-masted ships fully rigged on each mast and armed with 24-38 guns on a single gundeck. However, they were built with a sleeker, "clean" **run**, designed to enable the ships to move through the water faster. This feature made these vessels faster than the East Indiamen vessels.

Frigates were often compared with larger **ships of the line** in terms of how they handled in the water. These new merchant ships were compared with East Indiamen in the same way, so they were called Blackwall Frigates. Designed for efficiency, safety, speed,

and distance, they were often built with Burmese teak, a wood particularly well-suited for ships because of its strength and ability to resist rot.

Three companies—Green and Wigram, T. and W. Smith, and Duncan Dunbar—built these boats. The first of the Blackwall Frigates was Green and Wigram's *Seringapatam*. Built in 1837, she was an 818-ton **packet-ship** that was 152 feet, 6 inches long, and 34 feet, 6 inches in the **beam**. Years later, Robert Wigram would say she was "the first of a new class, and was a great advance in size and form on previous vessels." Her form was actually much the same as standard warships of the day. However, she was clearly an advance in size; the largest ship previously built at the Blackwall Yard had been 656 tons.

The *Seringapatam* was a fast, reliable ship. She set a new record of 85 days for the London to Bombay run, acquired a reputation for speed, and was the model for 12 more Blackwall Frigates.

Blackwall Frigates were the primary ships used in trade between England and India, Australia, and New Zealand. After the Suez Canal opened in 1869, the use of Blackwall Frigates diminished. They were gradually replaced by the even faster American clipper ships, but many continued to sail, transporting wool from Australia to England.

26. Archimedes
1838

The earliest ships were propelled by oar and sail. They were dependent on the strength and stamina of the people rowing, and the presence of wind to fill their sails. Mechanical propulsion eliminated both oar and sail, and drove ships faster, in any kind of water or weather.

The first means of mechanical propulsion was a steam-driven paddle-wheel that functioned as a mechanical set of oars. The most common paddle-wheel designs are **side-wheeler** and **stern-wheeler**. While paddle-wheelers functioned well in rivers (see no. 34), they had problems in rough seas because rough water made ships roll, or move from side to side. When a stern-wheeler rolled, its paddle came out of the water; when a side-wheeler rolled, one paddle was out of the water and useless, and the other became more deeply submerged and under severe strain. The solution to this problem was a means of mechanical propulsion that would always be submerged. To achieve this, ship designers mounted a propeller on a constantly turning screw that was placed under the ship. Turned by the ship's engines, the spinning propeller was always submerged because it was beneath the vessel, and provided the thrust that would move a ship forward.

Four men, working separately, developed the screw propeller between 1833 and 1836. On May 31, 1836, an Englishman named Francis Pettit Smith was awarded a patent for the new device.

The Archimedes

The first large ocean-going vessel to be powered by the screw propeller was the *Archimedes*. Designed by Smith, and built at Millwall on the Thames for the Ship Propeller Company, the *Archimedes* was launched in November 1838. Smith had previously constructed a small ten-ton propeller-driven ship; the *Archimedes* was built to demonstrate the effectiveness of screw propulsion on a larger vessel. A three-masted schooner, the *Archimedes* displaced 237 tons, had a length of 106 feet, and was 22 feet across the **beam**. Her propeller screw was 5 feet, 9 inches in diameter and was turned by a 90-horsepower steam engine. She could make a speed of up to 10 knots.

The *Archimedes* did indeed prove how effective screw propulsion was; she easily sliced through the waters around Britain and steamed on to Portugal. In 1840 the engineer Isambard Kingdom Brunel chartered her for six months so he could study this new means of power. Brunel was so impressed that he used screw propulsion for the *Great Britain* (see no. 28), a ship he was building as a paddle steamer.

However, the *Archimedes* had a fate similar to that of the *Savannah*. (see no. 23). Although the *Archimedes* demonstrated the effectiveness of the screw propeller and ushered in a new era, she finished her days as a sailing vessel, plying the trade routes between South America and Australia.

The Great Western

represented a new level of luxury travel.

The *Great Western* left dry dock on July 19, 1837. Her first trans-Atlantic crossing began on April 8, 1838. On her maiden voyage, from Bristol, England, to New York, she carried 24 first-class passengers and crossed the Atlantic in 15 days at an average speed of eight knots. When she arrived in New York on April 23, 1838, the *Great Western* still had 200 tons of coal on board, which was 25 percent of her fuel; this demonstrated that, with the right design, a steam-powered vessel could easily carry enough fuel for a long trip.

While the *Great Western* was being completed, its builders had developed a race with a rival company to see who would begin the first scheduled trans-Atlantic steamship service. The other ship, a packet-steamer named the *Sirius*, left Ireland on April 4, 1838. Even with this four-day head start, the *Sirius* arrived in New York only four hours before the *Great Western*.

The *Great Western* crossed the Atlantic for another eight years, making a total of 67 problem-free trips and establishing a typical crossing-time of 12 days, 6 hours. She then began a ten-year career carrying cargo and passengers between Southampton, England, and the West Indies. The *Great Western* was dismantled in 1856.

One of the great names associated with shipbuilding in the 19th century is Isambard Kingdom Brunel, the engineer remembered for his vision, innovation and three spectacular vessels he designed, the first of which was the *Great Western*.

Designed by Brunel and built by William Patterson, the *Great Western* was created so Britain's Great Western Railway could offer its passengers service not only through England, but across the Atlantic Ocean as well. She was the first steam-powered vessel to ply the Atlantic on a regular basis.

The largest steam-driven ship of her time, the *Great Western* was a 1,340-ton wooden vessel, 236 feet long and 35 feet across the **beam**. She had four boilers and a 750-horsepower two-cylinder engine that drove two paddle-wheels. Her boilers and engine were so large they took up half the boat's interior space. The paddle-wheels were each 28 feet, 9 inches in diameter, and one was mounted on each side of the ship. The *Great Western* could also be powered by sails, which she carried on four masts. She had the capacity to carry 148 passengers, and her speed was nine knots. She

The *Great Britain* was the first large iron ship created to be a trans-Atlantic passenger vessel, and the first iron ship to be powered by a screw propeller. The second great ship built by the famous 19th century ship-builder, Isambard Kingdom Brunel, she was also the largest ship of her day.

The launch of the Great Britain

With the *Great Britain* came a number of other innovations. Her **hull** was stronger than those of other ships and was divided into six sections separated by water-tight **bulkheads**, making her the first vessel to use such structures for safety. She also had **bilge keels** to support the weight of the ship during launching and while in dry-dock for maintenance, and to provide resistance and stability in heavy seas.

The *Great Britain* displaced 3,270 tons, was 322 feet long, 50 feet across the **beam**, and had one **funnel**. Her four-cylinder 1,500-horsepower engine and four-bladed propeller gave her a speed of 12 knots. She also carried six masts and her sails totaled 15,300 square feet. She had cabin space for 360 passengers.

The *Great Britain* was launched from Bristol, England on July 19, 1843. She made her first trip, from Liverpool, England, to New York in August 1845. The ship carried 60 first-class passengers and a large number of additional passengers in **steerage**. She also had 600 tons of cargo on board. She made the crossing in slightly less than 15 days.

The *Great Britain* plied the Atlantic for another year, but in 1846 ran aground on rocks in Dundrum Bay off the coast of Ireland. She remained stranded for the next 11 months, pounded by the sea. Any other ship of the era would have been destroyed, but when she was finally refloated, she required only minor repairs. At this time she was also reconfigured to have two funnels and four masts.

Over the next 30 years, the *Great Britain* served as a passenger and cargo transport between England and Australia. On one trip she carried more than 600 people. In 1866 she was caught in a vicious gale off Cape Horn. She was beached at Port Stanley in the Falkland Islands, where she became a coal hulk, left stationary, and used to store coal.

More than a century passed, and then in 1970, the *Great Britain* was refloated and towed to Montevideo, Uruguay. From there she was towed back home to Bristol, where she was put into the same dry dock in which she had been built 127 years earlier. During the late 1990s, she was in the process of being restored, and was open to the public for viewing.

The yacht America

Yachts were originally ships of state that carried important people, such as ambassadors or princes, from one kingdom to another. Later the term came to designate ships powered by sail or engine that were used for pleasure as opposed to commerce.

One of the most famous yachts in history is the America. She had a long, varied career, during which she was a warship and a pleasure craft, but she began as a racing yacht. Built specifically to race in British waters, she was a 170-ton, 110-foot-long schooner. She was constructed in New York in 1851 by George Steers, who created her for John Stevens, commodore of the New York Yacht Club. On August 22, 1851, the America took part in a race around the Isle of Wight, off the south coast of England, and finished first among 16 ships. The Royal Yacht Squadron presented her with a cup that has since been known as the America's Cup. It is the most prized trophy in international pleasure racing. Since 1851, there have been 29 competitions for the America's Cup.

During the late 1850s, the *America* was sold, rebuilt with English oak, and renamed the *Camilla*. By 1861, she'd found her way to Savannah, Georgia, and during the U.S. Civil War she served the Confederacy. During this period, guns were mounted on her deck, and she was used as a blockade runner. While being pursued by Union ships, she was **scuttled** by her crew in Florida's St. John's River to avoid being captured. She was later raised and became part of the Union Navy. For a while she was called *Memphis*, but her original name was soon restored. As *America*, she participated in the blockade of Charleston, South Carolina.

Following the Civil War, she served as a training ship at the U.S. Naval Academy at Annapolis, Maryland, and in 1870 she was recommissioned as a yacht. On August 8 of that year, the English made their first bid to capture the America's Cup. The *America* took part in this race and finished fourth, beating the English challenger by 13 minutes. The race was won by the American schooner *Magic*.

Sold in 1873, *America* became a cruising yacht and raced only occasionally. In 1917 she was sold again. With World War I raging, her lead keel was removed and donated to the war effort. In 1921 she was sold for $1, to be preserved at Annapolis.

In March 1942, the roof of her shed collapsed in a severe snow storm, and her timbers were damaged so badly that they could not be repaired. She was broken up in 1945, but her legacy lives on in the America's Cup race.

The *Great Eastern* was the most advanced and ambitious of the three great ships built by the great visionary engineer Isambard Kingdom Brunel.

After four years of construction, the *Great Eastern* was launched on January 31, 1858. Compared to the other vessels of her time, the *Great Eastern* was truly a giant. Most ships of the day were under 5,000 tons, but the *Great Eastern* had a tonnage of 18,914. She had five **funnels** and was designed to carry 4,000 passengers. If used as a troopship, she could transport 10,000 soldiers. With the capacity to store 12,200 tons of coal, she could carry 6,000 tons of cargo from England to Australia or India without having to refuel.

The *Great Eastern* was 692 feet long and 82 feet across the **beam**; for more than 40 years she was the largest ship in the world. She had a top speed of 15 knots and was powered by a 3,410-horsepower four-cylinder

only ship ever built with sails, paddles and a screw propeller.

A master of "firsts," Brunel built the *Great Eastern* as the first vessel to have a separate steering engine, and the first ship to have a cellular double bottom to prevent it from sinking if the ship's **hull** tears open. Her superb construction was clearly demonstrated when she ran onto a rock and came away with only slight damage.

Ironically, although the *Great Eastern* was the most luxurious liner of her day, ultimately she was a failure as a ship and for Brunel. Problems during construction and delays in launching caused the financial ruin of the ship's builder, John Scott Russell, and the project became so stressful that it ruined Brunel's health. Two days before the *Great Eastern* was scheduled to make her first voyage, Brunel suffered a stroke. He died ten days later.

The Great Eastern

The *Great Eastern* was plagued by problems throughout her existence. Originally designed for the India or Australia route, she was put into passenger service on the Atlantic, where she lost money for her owners. In 1864 she was sold at auction.

Taken out of service as a passenger liner, she was converted to a cable carrier, and was finally put to good use laying the first trans-Atlantic cable in 1866. She also laid three other trans-Atlantic

engine that turned two paddle-wheels 56 feet in diameter—the largest paddle-wheels ever mounted on an ocean liner. She also had a 24-foot four-bladed propeller powered by a 4,890-horsepower engine. Her six masts carried 58,500 square feet of sail. She was the

cables as well as one Indian Ocean cable from Aden to Bombay.

The *Great Eastern* ended her days as a showboat in Liverpool. In 1888 she was beached at New Ferry, England, where she was dismantled.

David Glasgow Farragut (1801–1870) was the Union naval captain remembered for having said, "Damn the torpedoes, full speed ahead." He gave this famous order aboard his **flagship**, the *Hartford*, during the American Civil War battle to capture Mobile Bay in Alabama.

The *Hartford* was launched at the Boston Navy Yard in November 1858. Work on the ship was completed while she was berthed, and she was ready for service in June 1859. A wooden-hulled **sloop**, she displaced 2,900 tons, and was 225 feet long and 44 feet across the **beam**. In addition to her sails, she had auxiliary steam power. Her light, efficient engines burned less coal than other steam engines, and could drive her at 9.5 knots in good weather. The *Hartford* initially served in the Far East, but when the Civil War began she returned home and was refitted. By 1862 she was armed with 20 nine-inch guns and two 20-pound rifles.

After the Union side captured New Orleans, Louisiana, on April 26, 1862, Mobile, Alabama, became the Confederacy's main port. Farragut wanted to attack Mobile after the fall of Vicksburg in 1863, but he was ordered to wait for seven months while the North built new **ironclad** vessels. On August 5, 1864, Farragut was ready to fight his way into Mobile Bay.

Before Farragut's fleet of 18 Union ships could engage the Confederate ironclads defending Mobile, it had to pass Fort Morgan at the entrance of the bay. Farragut had four ironclads, which could better withstand artillery fire, so he sent them nearest the fort, with the *Tecumseh* in the lead. He divided his 14 remaining wooden ships into two columns, with the seven smaller ships lashed alongside and protected by the seven larger ships, lead by the *Brooklyn*.

The *Tecumseh* hit a mine (which at that time were called torpedoes) and sank. Seeing this, the captain of the *Brooklyn* stopped and the ships behind her, including the *Hartford*, started steaming too close to the *Brooklyn*. Farragut ordered the *Hartford* to change course, but this put her in the path of other mines. When his command was questioned by his crew, he shouted his famous command.

During the three-hour battle, Farragut destroyed or captured the Confederate ships opposing him and took control of Mobile Bay. To honor him, Congress created the rank of vice admiral; previously, the U.S. Navy had no rank above rear admiral.

After the Civil War, the *Hartford* remained active. She was refitted again in 1880 and given new machinery. After a third refit in 1887, she served as a training vessel before being permanently berthed at Norfolk Navy Yard. Here, on November 20, 1958, the *Hartford* finally met her end when she sank in her berth.

Farragut in the rigging of the Hartford

32. Monitor / Merrimack (Virginia)
1862

The *Monitor* and the *Merrimack* will forever be linked in history as the ships that faced each other in the first duel between **ironclads**. Ironclads came into use in 1853 after a battle between Turkish and Russian vessels at Sinope on the southern coast of the Black Sea demonstrated the vulnerability of wooden ships to artillery fire. The first true ironclad was the French frigate *Gloire* (1859). The first battleship made entirely of iron was Britain's *Warrior* (1860).

The American Civil War ironclad *Monitor* was a Union ship designed by John Ericsson and hastily built in New York in 1862. The North had learned that the South was converting the captured Union ship *Merrimack* to an ironclad, and needed an armored vessel of its own to respond to this threat. Weighing 978 tons, the *Monitor* was 172 feet long and 41 feet, 6 inches across the **beam**. She had a shallow **draught**, a low **freeboard**, and mounted two 11-inch guns in a revolving turret. Her armor consisted of eight-inch-thick iron plates on her turret and five-inch-thick iron plates on her **hull**. People ridiculed her low freeboard and turret configuration, calling her a "cheesebox on a raft." While this design made her a difficult target for enemy ships, the *Monitor* was a slow vessel able to make only four knots; she almost sank twice while on her way to engage the *Merrimack*.

The *Merrimack* was one of six vessels authorized by Congress in 1854 that were named after American rivers. A 40-gun sailing ship with an auxiliary steam engine, she was 275 feet long, 51 feet across the **beam**, and displaced 4,650 tons. **Scuttled** by Northern forces when they retreated from Norfolk,

Clash of the ironclads

Virginia, in April 1861, she was taken by the Confederacy and renamed the *Virginia*. The South reworked her machinery, made her an ironclad, and armed her with ten guns and an iron ram. Southern shipbuilders also added a sloping wooden **casemate** covered with four-inch-thick iron plates across her deck.

The *Monitor* and *Merrimack* fought their famous battle at Hampton Roads, Virginia, on March 9, 1862. The close engagement lasted four hours, but neither ship suffered serious damage. Finally, the *Merrimack* withdrew; neither vessel emerged victorious.

A month after her engagement with the *Monitor*, the *Merrimack* returned to Hampton Roads but did not enter into combat. On May 11, 1862, the *Merrimack*'s crew destroyed her when the Confederacy evacuated Norfolk.

The *Monitor* went on to serve on the James River but foundered off Cape Hatteras on December 31, 1862. Her name "monitor" has come to designate a class of naval vessels: low freeboard, shallow-**draught** ships with one or two large turret-mounted guns, that are used for bombardment of coastal positions. The English built many *monitors* during World War I, and they were also used in World War II.

33. Cutty Sark
1869

During the mid 19th century, discovery of gold in California and Australia, and increasing trade between China and Europe, created a demand for ships that could cross oceans quickly. Consequently, the mid-1800s became the heyday of the clipper ship.

Clippers were sailing ships built for speed and maneuverability. They used a new **hull** design that was long and low, with a narrow, inward-curving **bow** that sliced through the water like a knife. This decreased the hull area that came into contact with the water, increasing a ship's speed.

The term "clipper" was first used to describe the fast American-designed ships that distinguished themselves in the War of 1812. However, the first true clipper ship was considered to be the *Rainbow*, built in New York in 1845. It is believed these ships got their name because they "clipped" the time other boats needed for ocean voyages. British shipbuilders began building clippers too, and they eventually replaced the Blackwall frigates.

One of the most famous clipper ships— and the only surviving British tea clipper, originally built to carry tea to England—was the *Cutty Sark*, launched at Dumbarton, Scotland, in November 1869. Weighing 963 tons, the *Cutty Sark* was 212 feet long and 36 feet across the **beam**. She carried a crew of 35. Many clippers were composite-built—

The Cutty Sark, 1922

wood over metal; the hull of the *Cutty Sark* was an iron frame covered with elm and teak. The bottom of her hull was protected with copper. She had three masts, and her main mast was 145 feet tall.

Built in the closing days of the clipper era, the *Cutty Sark* made only eight trips carrying tea between India and England. The opening of the Suez Canal in 1869 marked the beginning of the end for clipper ships. In 1883, the *Cutty Sark* was put into service carrying wool from Australia to England and taking emigrants from England to Australia. During this time, she became famous for some extremely fast runs. The last of these was during 1894–1895, after which she was sold to Portuguese owners and renamed the *Ferreira*.

In 1922, she was bought and restored by an English sea captain. From 1936-1949 she was a training ship. In 1954, she was placed in a specially constructed dock in Greenwich, London. Three years later she was completely restored and became a public museum.

"Cutty Sark" is a Scottish term for a short dress. The name *Cutty Sark* comes from the poem "Tam O'Shanter" by Scottish poet Robert Burns. In the poem, a farmer is chased by a young witch named Nannie. The *Cutty Sark's* figurehead is a carving of Nannie in her cutty sark, with her arm reaching out to catch the tail of the horse ridden by the farmer.

Rotating paddles were used to power boats as far back as the time of the ancient Egyptians. When the steam engine was developed, steam-powered paddle-wheels were added. As steam paddle boats evolved, the most common configurations were two paddle **side-wheelers** and one paddle **stern-wheelers.** (see no. 26)

Steam had clear advantages over sail, but there were disadvantages to paddle-wheels on the open ocean. In bad weather and rough seas, paddles could get damaged. Fully-loaded cargo vessels sat low in the water, deeply immersing the paddle-wheels and making them less efficient.

However, paddle-wheels had definite advantages on rivers and lakes, especially in shallow waterways with shoals and sandbars. Paddle-wheels could generate as much propulsion going forward or backward, which made them highly maneuverable when stopping or docking.

During the 19th century, the paddle steamer was in its glory. Handsome stern-wheelers and side-wheelers plied American rivers, transporting people and cargo up and down the growing nation's waterways. Some steamboats weighed as much as 5,000 tons. They had as many as five or six decks built over a flat **hull** that tapered to a point at the front of the ship. These larger boats had 40-foot paddle-wheels turned by steam that was generated by a boiler set on the same deck as the paddle shaft.

Two of the most well-known side-wheelers were the *Robert E. Lee* and the *Natchez.* The most famous Mississippi River steamboat—the *Robert E. Lee*—was built at New Albany, Indiana, in 1866. She was 300

feet long, 44 feet wide, weighed 1,467 tons and drew steam from eight boilers. Captained by John W. Cannon, her home port was New Orleans, Louisiana.

The *Natchez* was built in Cincinnati, Ohio, in 1869. She weighed 1,547 tons, was 301 feet, 5 inches long, measured 42 feet, 5 inches across the **beam** and carried eight boilers. Her captain was Thomas P. Leathers. Her home port was also New Orleans, and she was considered one of the fastest boats on the Mississippi.

In 1870, the *Natchez* and the *Robert E. Lee* raced about 1,218 miles up the Mississippi from New Orleans to St. Louis, Missouri. The competition riveted people all over the United States and Europe, and became one of the most famous races in American history. Bets on the outcome totaled more than one million dollars. The *Robert E. Lee* won the race, reaching St. Louis in three days, eighteen hours and fourteen minutes, a record that was never matched by another paddle-wheeler. The *Natchez* arrived six and one-half hours later.

Paddle steamers are still with us in some form today. They are usually used as ferries or tourist attractions on rivers, and in recent years, many of them have been turned into floating casinos.

The Robert E. Lee

The Devastation

In the days of sailing ships, what we know today as the battleship was called the **ship of the line** (see no. 12). The transition from the wooden ship of the line to the modern battleship was gradual; at times battleships were a combination of old and new designs. Early ships of the line were sailing ships made of wood. Later, wooden ships were plated with metal and called ironclads. The next generation of ships were made entirely of iron and finally, steel. In addition to having iron added to their wood **hulls**, sailing ships were lengthened so they could be powered by steam engines. The first ships to be built entirely of iron still carried sails on masts and mounted the same artillery batteries of the older sailing ships.

As engines and weaponry developed and improved, the battleship came in to its own as a separate, clearly recognizable class of ship. The first battleships to be powered entirely by steam were called mastless ships. The first British battleship driven solely by steam was the *Devastation*.

The *Devastation* was an iron-hulled ship weighing 9,330 tons. Designed in 1869, launched in July 1871, and completed dockside in 1873, the *Devastation* was 285 feet long and 65 feet, 3 inches across the **beam**. She had one turret forward and one **aft**, each mounting two 12-inch guns that could penetrate 15-inch iron from a distance of 1,000 yards. She had a very low **freeboard**, no **forecastle**, and no **poop deck**. Her steam engines drove two four-bladed screw propellers. The vessel had the capacity to carry a huge amount of coal—as much as 1,600 tons—and operating at five knots she had a range of 9,200 miles. She had only one mast and did not carry sails.

The *Devastation* had excellent protection from enemy fire. The total weight of her armor was more than 3,000 tons, and her hull was divided into watertight compartments. Originally, she was built with an open passage on each side of the main deck to allow the crew to get from one end of the ship to the other. However, this did not provide full protection for her crew, so the passage was covered with a **superstructure** that extended to the sides of the ship and half-way to the stern. The rear of the superstructure was designed with a recess so her aft guns could fire over the stern on a downward angle.

The *Devastation* was refitted in 1879, and in 1892 she received newer, more advanced engines. A major step forward in warship design, the *Devastation* represented a transition to even better battleships. She was retired in 1902, and broken down in 1908.

36. **Holland**
1879

There were attempts to develop the submarine as early as 1578, but the right combination of technology and enthusiasm for underwater vessels would not come together for another 300 years. In 1801, Robert Fulton built and demonstrated the submarine *Nautilus* for Napoleon, but there was little official interest in his craft.

During the American Civil War, the Confederacy built several small, crude submersible ships called Davids. These vessels carried mounted spar torpedoes—explosive charges mounted on a long pole carried over the **bow**—and had to ram a ship in order to sink it. In the two recorded attacks by Davids, only one Union ship was sunk and two southern Davids were lost.

To work as an undersea vessel, a submarine requires a circular **hull** so it can withstand water pressure when submerged. It must also have **ballast tanks** so the vessel can submerge and resurface. In addition, a submarine must also have a horizontal rudder to control her depth and forward motion when underwater, and a propulsion system that can function without air when the vessel is submerged.

The American engineer J. P. Holland was the person who incorporated all the characteristics of a practical submarine in one vessel. His first successful design was the *Holland No. 1*, a small 2.2-ton ship launched in 1878. The *Holland No. 1* was an experimental ship. After successful testing, her engine was removed and she was sunk in the Upper Passaic River in New Jersey, although she was later raised.

Next came the *Holland*, which was launched at Elizabethport, New Jersey, in 1879. Displacing 105 tons on the surface, the *Holland* had a surface speed of 8.5 knots and a submerged speed of 7 knots. She was powered by a 45-horsepower gasoline engine for surface cruising and an electric motor for running underwater. Her range was 500 miles on

The Holland

the surface and 60 miles when submerged.

The first modern U.S. submarine was the *Holland VI*. Launched on May 17, 1897, she displaced 63 tons on the surface and 74 tons submerged. She was 53 feet, 3 inches long and 10 feet, 3 inches wide. Her surface speed was eight knots, and when submerged she made five knots. She had a 45-horsepower gasoline motor—like the *Holland*—and a 75-horsepower electric motor. The *Holland VI* had the ability to dive to a depth of 75 feet, had one torpedo tube in the center of her bow, and carried three torpedoes. She was bought by the U.S. Navy on April 11, 1900, commissioned on October 12, and designated the SS-1. The vessel was scrapped in 1913.

Today, replicas of the *Holland No. 1* and the *Holland* are on display at the Paterson Museum in Paterson, New Jersey.

Two of the most forbidding places in the world are the North and South Poles. These areas are especially hostile to ships because of huge ice floes and icebergs that can strand ships or crush them to pieces. Yet one ship, the *Fram*, has earned her place in history specifically because of journeys she made across both the Arctic Circle and Antarctica.

The *Fram* was a 402-ton, three-masted schooner fitted with an auxiliary steam engine. She was designed by the Norwegian polar explorer and scientist Fridtjof Nansen, and was the first vessel specifically designed to withstand winter in polar ice. Her **hull** was specially reinforced and semicircular in shape so that no matter how much pressure ice exerted on her, she would be raised free. In addition, she had two watertight **bulkheads**. As a further precaution, the vessel was equipped with eight smaller boats. If she were wrecked, two of these boats could carry her small crew and the supplies they needed to survive.

Explorer Roald Amundsen

The *Fram* took Nansen safely across the Arctic Ocean on a three-year journey from 1893 to 1896. Nansen believed that a polar current flowed toward the east coast of Greenland. To test his theory, he allowed the *Fram* to simply drift with the flow of arctic ice, in the direction of the North Pole. When she had drifted as far north as Nansen thought the current would take her, he left the *Fram* in the care of its captain, Otto Sverdrup, while he continued on land, traveling by sled and going farther north than anyone had ever ventured before.

During 1898–1902, the *Fram* took Sverdrup on an expedition above the Arctic Circle to explore the islands northwest of Greenland.

The *Fram*'s most famous journey occurred in 1910, when she sailed to the bottom of the world, taking the Norwegian explorer Roald Amundsen (1872–1928) to the Antarctic. Amundsen initially decided to repeat Nansen's northward drift and become the first person to reach the North Pole. The Norwegian government gave him the *Fram* for the trip.

However, after the American explorer Admiral Robert E. Peary reached the North Pole in April 1909, Amundsen decided to be the first person to reach the South Pole. The *Fram* took him as far south as a ship could go. Then Amundsen and four other explorers used dogs and sleds to travel a new, never-used overland route. On December 14, 1911, they became the first people to reach the South Pole.

The *Fram* is now a Norwegian national monument, preserved in her own specially built museum near Oslo, Norway.

"Remember the *Maine!*" has become one of the most famous battle cries in U.S. history. During the Spanish-American War, it stirred U.S. citizens and soldiers to action.

Commissioned in 1895, the *Maine* was a 6,682-ton American battleship, 318 feet long and 21 feet, 6 inches across the **beam**. She was armed with six six-inch guns and four ten-inch guns, her top speed was 16.4 knots, and she carried a crew of 354.

The ship had two **military masts**, but was powered by twin screw propellers driven by triple expansion engines. The first steam engines were single-cylinder engines. Next came the improved two-cylinder compound engine. In the compound engine, after steam left the first cylinder it passed through a second cylinder, where it was changed back to water, and was then sent to the boiler. Using the steam twice added to the engine's thrust and gave more power using the same amount of steam. The triple expansion engine added a third cylinder and used the steam three times instead of twice, generating even more power.

On January 24, 1898, the *Maine* was sent to Havana, Cuba, with orders to protect the lives and property of U.S. citizens there. Riots had been taking place in the Cuban capital as Cubans continued their battle to gain freedom from Spanish rule.

At 9:40 p.m. on February 15, 1898, as the *Maine* lay at anchor in Havana Harbor, there were two explosions. The first was a solid thud; the second was a much bigger blast.

The *Maine* was split in half and blown into pieces that flew as high as 200 feet into the air. The blast killed 260 of the 329 seamen and soldiers on the ship, and the *Maine* went to the bottom of the harbor.

There were two investigations, one by American officials, the other by Spanish authorities. The Spanish claimed the blast was caused by an accidental explosion aboard the ship, and suggested spontaneous combustion in the coal storage areas because gunpowder

The Maine

had been stored nearby. However, the American investigation concluded that the ship had been struck by a mine or a torpedo, which caused the forward magazine to explode.

In the United States, the sinking of the *Maine* caused an uproar. People blamed Spain for sinking the ship and newspapers screamed, *"Remember the Maine, to hell with Spain."* Within two months, America was at war with Spain.

In 1911, a section of the *Maine's* **hull** was brought up and a new American investigation was conducted. This second inquiry came to the same conclusion as the first—the ship had been sunk by sabotage. However, the exact cause of the *Maine's* destruction remains a mystery to this day.

In 1897, a new type of engine was introduced that revolutionized how ships were powered—the turbine. The turbine delivers a powerful blast of steam that turns blades that are set in a circular configuration in a drum. As the blades spin, they turn the drum, which is connected to a shaft that turns the ship's propeller.

Before the turbine, the reciprocating engine was in common use. In the reciprocating engine, a piston moved inside a cylinder, and this motion was transferred to the propeller shaft through a connecting rod. Turbines were simpler and more efficient than reciprocating engines.

The turbine was invented by the English engineer Charles Parsons in 1884, but was not immediately used to power ships. Instead, it was first used for ships' lighting systems; then Parsons applied his invention to power stations. It wasn't until 1894 that Parsons turned his attention to using the turbine engine for the propulsion of boats.

To demonstrate this use of his engine, Parsons designed the yacht *Turbinia*. Built in 1894, the *Turbinia* was a small steel vessel that was 100 feet long, 9 feet in the **beam**, and had a **draft** of 3 feet. She displaced 44.5 tons. The *Turbinia* was powered by three turbine engines that developed 2,000 horsepower and turned three shafts. Each shaft had three screw propellers.

The *Turbinia* was unveiled to the public at the Diamond Jubilee Review of the British Navy at Spithead, off England, on June 26, 1897. A celebration to commemorate 60 years of rule by Queen Victoria, this was an enormous gathering of ships from all over the world—the perfect setting for Parsons to show what his new engine could accomplish.

Included in the array of ships were 165 vessels from the Royal Navy. Among these were six sailing **brigs**, survivors of a bygone era. The other English ships were all modern — powered by reciprocating engines. But by the end of the day, these, too, would belong to a bygone era of marine propulsion.

The *Turbinia* was indeed impressive. Appearing suddenly as if out of thin air, she roared around the anchored ships of navies from all over the world at an average speed of 30 knots (her top speed was 34.5 knots), far beyond the boats of her day. During this demonstration, a naval steam launch tried to catch her but could not.

Engineers, shipbuilders, and naval officials were so awed by the *Turbinia's* performance that they soon began using turbines instead of reciprocating engines. Bigger turbine-powered ships would later be built, but until they were, the *Turbinia* was the fastest ship in the world.

The Turbinia

At 10:35 a.m. on Thursday, December 17, 1903, the age of engine-powered airplane flight was born in the air over Kitty Hawk, North Carolina. Two brothers will forever be linked with this momentous event—Wilbur and Orville Wright, the designers and builders of the airplane called *Flyer*.

Flyer was a **biplane**. It had a wingspan of 40 feet, 4 inches and an overall length of 21, feet 1 inch. Empty, it weighed 605 pounds. Powered by a 12-horsepower, four-cylinder, water-cooled engine with two chain-driven propellers each eight feet, six inches in diameter, *Flyer* was launched using a dolly running on a 60-foot wooden rail. The aircraft's speed was about 30 mph. The pilot controlled the plane while lying on his stomach.

The Flyer's first successful flight

The Wright brothers built *Flyer* in the summer of 1903, but it wasn't perfected and ready to take to the air until December. This meant flying in freezing temperatures and powerful winds. The brothers first attempted a flight on December 14, launching their plane from a rail with a downward angle. They tossed a coin to determine who would pilot the plane, and Wilbur won. The plane lifted off the ground; however, he climbed too steeply, and after being in the air for only three-and-a-half seconds, *Flyer* stalled and crashed. The landing gear was damaged, and the brothers spent the next two days repairing the plane. Meanwhile, the wind continued to blow hard.

On December 17, the wind was still blowing at 25 mph, and rain had left puddles that had turned to ice. However, the Wrights remained determined to take to the air. This time the take-off rail was level. With Orville as pilot, the plane taxied down the rail; Wilbur ran next to it, holding the wings to keep it level. Hitting the end of the rail at about seven to eight mph, Orville and *Flyer* went aloft, remaining airborne for about 12 seconds in a wavering flight that covered 120 feet. Then the plane veered sharply toward the ground and landed softly on the sand.

Orville proclaimed it "the first [flight] in the history of the world in which a machine carrying a man had raised itself by its own power into the air in full flight, and sailed forward without reduction of speed, and had finally landed at a point as high as that from which it started."

The brothers made three more flights that day (covering distances of 175 feet, 200 feet, and 852 feet) with Wilbur and Orville alternating as pilots. Wilbur was the pilot for the last flight, during which the plane was once again damaged, this time requiring major repairs.

Today, the *Flyer* is on display at the National Air and Space Museum in Washington, D.C.

Like the British ship the *Bounty* (see no. 18), the *Potemkin*'s fame stems from a mutiny that took place aboard the ship. The battleship *Potemkin* (its full name was *Kniaz Potemkin Tavricheski*) was part of Russia's Black Sea Fleet during the first decade of the 20th century. The mutiny with which it will always be associated took place on June 25, 1905.

Commissioned in 1904, the *Potemkin* displaced 12,548 tons. She had two heavy gun turrets, one forward and one **aft**, and was armed with four 12-inch guns. In her day, she was one of the Russian navy's most advanced ships.

First Officer, Ippolit Giliarovsky, viewed this refusal as mutiny, and in accordance with a long-standing Russian naval custom, he decreed that members of the crew should be selected at random and shot.

The sailors on the *Potemkin* who were ordered to execute their fellow crewmen refused to fire. Chaos followed; a sailor was shot and killed. The crew became enraged at Giliarovsky and killed him. By the time the mutiny was over, the captain, Eugene Golikov, and several other officers were dead.

The *Potemkin* returned to the port at Odessa, where the sailor's body was shown to the public. There was widespread rioting, during which 6,000 people were killed. Many of these deaths occurred in one incident, when Cossacks— Russia's cavalry— charged into a crowd, killing people at random.

The *Potemkin* left Odessa and roamed the Black

The officers and crew of the Potemkin

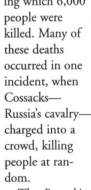

In February, 1904, Russia went to war with Japan; by the end of the year, it was clear that the war was not going well for Russia. In January 1905, its troops were forced to surrender a major Russian naval base at Port Arthur, China. There was discontent among the Russian people and the military, and talk of revolution against the czarist government.

Many different conditions contribute to a mutiny, and the spark that ignited the actual violence on the *Potemkin* is believed to have been bad meat. The crew, which already felt mistreated, refused to eat the meat. The ship's

Sea, looking for a port where she would be welcome. Unable to find a haven, her crew **scuttled** the ship in the harbor of Constanza, Rumania, in July 1905. She was later raised and refitted, and on October 9, 1905, renamed the *Panteleimon*.

In 1917 her original name was restored. A month later, she was given a third name— *Boretz zu Svobodu,* ("Fighter for Liberty"). During World War I, she saw action as both the *Potemkin* and the *Boretz zu Svobodu.* In 1923, this mighty battleship that had such a tumultuous career was dismantled.

Huge pleasure cruise ships were a common sight by the mid 20th century, but there was a time not too long before then that such ships did not exist. The idea of crossing the Atlantic Ocean in comfort and luxury did not arise until the early 20th century, when German businessman Albert Ballin, manager of the Hamburg-America Line, thought of sending a "hotel" to sea. To accomplish this, he built the *Auguste Victoria*—the first of what would come to be known as "floating palaces."

Named for the German Kaiser Wilhelm's wife, the 24,581-ton *Auguste Victoria* ushered in the age of modern sea travel. She was 705 feet long, 77 feet wide, and driven by powerful, advanced steam engines. She had a cruising speed of 17.5 knots, and could accommodate 2,996 passengers—652 in first class, 286 in second class, 216 in third class, and 1,842 in **steerage**.

Ballin added an innovative second propeller to his new ship that helped end crippling ocean breakdowns and was incorporated into future liners. In addition to making his passengers safer, Ballin wanted to provide for their every comfort. Rather than design the *Auguste Victoria* as just a boat, he set out to create a hotel, and hired architects famous for creating elegant resorts. The *Auguste Victoria* was decorated with Italian marble, African woods, stone, brass, ironwork, plants—even silver and gold. The ship had huge arched ceilings and gleaming chandeliers, and contained different rooms for different activities, such as a smoking room, a reading room, and salons where people gathered to socialize. The vessel even contained sweeping staircases on which people could make grand entrances.

Ballin also considered the passengers traveling in the poorest accommodations, those in steerage. The *Auguste Victoria* was the first ship on which meals were served in steerage. Sometimes people in steerage arrived in the

Albert Ballin

United States sick and were sent back to Europe. In 1910 Ballin addressed this problem by building a village in Hamburg, Germany, where as many as 5,000 immigrants could stay while waiting to sail. Ballin wanted to save his company the losses incurred when sick immigrants were sent back at the company's expense; by creating this village, it was easier for the company to monitor the health and welfare of the immigrants about to sail for America. Immigration became a major part of the company's business, providing half its profits.

Over the next several decades, Germany, England and France would engage in a highly competitive race to build bigger, faster, and more luxurious ships. With the birth of the *Auguste Victoria*, traveling across the ocean became more than just a sea voyage—it became like being a guest at a fine, floating hotel.

The name *Dreadnought* was used nine times in the history of the English Navy. The most famous *Dreadnought* was the eighth ship to bear this name, and she changed battleships forever.

During the late 1890s, the typical battleship carried four big guns, about ten smaller

The Dreadnought

guns, and various quick-firing guns as a defense against torpedo boats. These ships generally displaced about 10,000 tons and made speeds of about 16 knots.

However, naval battles during the Russo-Japanese War (1904–1905) revealed the disadvantages of arming ships with guns of different sizes. It became clear that big guns were most effective in combat at sea, and the next step was to create battleships that were "all big-gun."

Japan attempted to build the first all big-gun ship, the *Aki*, in the early days of the war, but never finished the ship. The U.S. and Russian navies were beginning to plan similar vessels, but it was England that succeeded in launching the first "all big gun" battleship.

A 17,900-ton battleship, the *Dreadnought* was built at Portsmouth, England, and

launched by Edward VII on February 10, 1906. She was 526 feet long and 26 feet, 3 inches across the **beam**. Carrying ten 12-inch guns set in five twin turrets, she was the world's first "all big gun" battleship and inaugurated a new era in battleship design and construction.

The *Dreadnought* was the first battleship powered by turbine engines. She had a top speed of 21 knots that made her the fastest warship of her day, and her big guns gave her more firepower than any other warship. She was protected by 8 to 11 inches of armor at the waterline and had 11-inch armor on her gun turrets. Her creator, Admiral Sir John Fisher, compared her to a hard-boiled egg, saying "she cannot be beat."

The *Dreadnought* was a new concept in naval architecture that immediately made every other battleship in the world, including all the others in the Royal Navy, obsolete. Her overwhelming superiority meant that every other navy had no choice but to adopt this new design.

The *Dreadnought* saw action throughout World War I, including ramming and sinking the German U-boat U-29 in 1915. However, in the "dreadnought race" to build bigger, faster and better-armed ships, the *Dreadnought* herself was soon outpaced by newer vessels. In 1920 she was sold and broken up.

Reflecting the contribution of this vessel, the term *dreadnought* came to designate a new class of modern battleships that were fast, well-armored, and equipped with large guns all of the same caliber.

44. Lusitania
1906

Less than 20 years after the sinking of the *Maine* was instrumental in bringing the United States into the Spanish-American War (see no. 38), the sinking of another vessel contributed to the United States entering World War I.

The British ocean liner *Lusitania* was launched in 1906. She was a 31,500-ton ship with four screws turned by turbine engines. At the time the largest ship in the world, the *Lusitania* was 761 feet long and 88 feet across the **beam**. On her maiden voyage in 1907, she crossed the Atlantic Ocean from Liverpool, England to New York at a speed of 23.99 knots, capturing the prestigious **Blue Riband** trophy.

Even after World War I began, she continued to cross the Atlantic every month. When she was about to depart New York on May 1, 1915, Germany issued warnings that ships flying the British flag were potential targets for submarines. However, the British did not take these warnings seriously. The *Lusitania* set sail as scheduled, with 1,959 passengers aboard.

On May 7, at 2:15 p.m., as the *Lusitania* approached the coast of Ireland she was hit in her **starboard** side by one or two torpedoes fired by the German submarine U-20. There were two explosions. The *Lusitania* began **listing** so badly that not all her lifeboats could be launched and she sank in less than 20 minutes. A total of 1,198 people lost their lives, including 124 Americans. The attack caused great outrage, particularly in the United States.

To this day there are different theories about exactly what happened. Because a state of war existed, the *Lusitania* should have been weaving a zigzag course and sailing at high speed. However, she was sailing straight, at a slower speed of 21 knots. It has been said that the British Admiralty did not send warnings of U-boat operations to the *Lusitania* as she neared Ireland. One theory claims she was deliberately not warned so she would be sunk, prompting the United States to enter the war on England's side.

Under international rules, an unarmed merchant ship could not be sunk without first determining that she was carrying war-related cargo, and then giving her an opportunity to ensure the safety of her passengers and crew. The *Lusitania* received no warning. However, it was later revealed that she was carrying war-related cargo— 5,000 cases of cartridges as well as other munitions. One theory suggested that the *Lusitania* was hit by one torpedo, and that the second explosion occurred when the cartridges blew up, causing the ship to sink so rapidly.

Germany's continuing policy of unrestricted submarine warfare was a major reason why the United States eventually entered World War I in 1917.

The Lusitania

The Wright brothers 1903 flight of their plane *Flyer* (see no. 40 had been witnessed by only a few people, and their claim that they had actually flown was met with skepticism. People refused to believe that a mechanically powered, heavier-than-air machine could fly.

The Wrights themselves had contributed to this situation. In 1902 they applied for a patent for their invention. However, until the patent was granted, they feared their ideas would be copied, so they worked in secrecy. Having finally achieved flight and obtained their patent, the

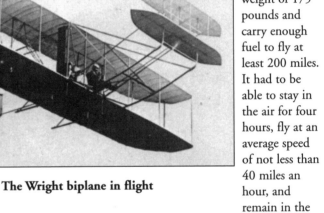

The Wright biplane in flight

Wright brothers faced the task of generating interest in their airplanes.

In the summer of 1908, they sent a plane to France and Wilbur traveled to Europe to conduct demonstrations for the French military. The Wrights' design and Wilbur's superb control of his aircraft greatly impressed the French and the British. French aircraft designer and aviator Louis Blériot, who in 1909 would become the first person to cross the English Channel in an airplane, declared, "A new era in mechanical flight has commenced."

Meanwhile, Orville conducted demonstrations for the U.S. Army at Fort Myer, Virginia. At one of these demonstrations on September 17, 1908, the plane piloted by

Orville crashed. Orville was badly injured and his passenger, Lieutenant Thomas E. Selfridge, became the world's first airplane fatality.

Nevertheless, military officials liked what they saw at Fort Myer. In October 1908, the U.S. Army drew up the first military specifications for an airplane. The aircraft was to accommodate two people with an average weight of 175 pounds and carry enough fuel to fly at least 200 miles. It had to be able to stay in the air for four hours, fly at an average speed of not less than 40 miles an hour, and remain in the air for the entire trial. At a time when flights were measured in feet rather than miles, and minutes instead of hours, these specifications were both demanding and daunting. However, on December 31, 1908, Wilbur Wright flew a biplane 77 miles in two hours and two minutes, breaking every flight record in existence, including all of his own.

On July 30, 1909, the U.S. Army purchased its first plane: the Wright biplane, *Miss Columbia*. The aircraft was priced at $25,000, but a bonus of $5,000 was added because in a test flight it surpassed the requested maximum speed of 40 mph. The Wright brothers had once again demonstrated their mastery of the skies, and the U.S. military had taken its first step into the air age.

46. Curtiss Hydroaeroplane
1911

Though the Wright brothers dominated the early days of aviation, especially in the United States, other pioneers were taking to the air and making ground-breaking contributions. One of these people was Glenn H. Curtiss. Curtiss became famous for racing bicycles and was an innovative designer of motorcycles. In 1907 he set a motorcycle record of 137 mph. He also belonged to the Aerial Experiment Association, founded in 1907 by Alexander Graham Bell.

One of Curtiss's main areas of interest was speed. He was constantly trying to perfect engines that would enable a plane to fly faster. Curtiss also focused on seaplanes; he gave more attention to marine aircraft than any other aviation pioneer, and has been called the "Father of Naval Aviation."

Others people had designed or built planes that could float on water. However, no one had been able to create a real seaplane—one that could take off from water, stay in the air, and land on water. After three years of experimentation, Curtiss built a **biplane** that had parts commonly found on boats.

Curtiss's biplane was equipped with **outriggers**. The undercarriage of the plane had two floats and elements that served as **hydrofoils**. The main float, which was under the **fuselage**, was 6 feet long and 5 feet wide. The smaller float was forward. The hydrofoils were also installed forward, beneath the outriggers, and helped lift the plane as it

made its take-off run. In addition, the hydrofoils helped the pilot control the plane while it reached flying speed.

On February 17, 1911, with Curtiss at the controls, the hydroaeroplane became the first aircraft to make a planned landing on water, taxi, and take off again. Curtiss landed his plane next to the cruiser *Pennsylvania*, which was at rest in the harbor at San Diego, California. To repeat the accomplishment of taking off from water, the plane was hoisted aboard the ship. Ten minutes later, it was lowered back into the water and Curtiss took off a second time. The "seaplane" had been born.

On July 1, 1911, a more developed Curtiss hydroaeroplane was purchased by the U.S. Navy. This model was called the *Triad* because it could function on land, in the air, and on the sea. The *Triad* had a large float

The Curtiss hydroaeroplane

between its wheels for use at sea; its retractable wheels were manually raised when taking off, and extended and locked into position for landing. Designated the A-1, the *Triad* was the U.S. Navy's first airplane.

53

Titanic
1911

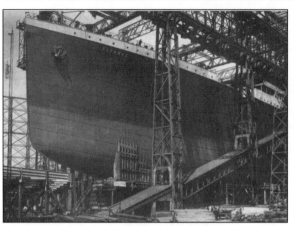

The Titanic under construction

Perhaps the most recognized name in maritime history is *Titanic*, the glorious "unsinkable" ocean liner that tragically sank on her maiden voyage.

The *Titanic* was aptly named. When she was built, she was the largest ship in the world. There was good reason to believe she was unsinkable. Built to standards that exceeded regulations, she had a double-bottom **hull** divided into 16 watertight compartments and could stay afloat even if as many as four of these compartments were breached.

The *Titanic* was launched on May 31, 1911. She was 883 feet long and 92 feet, 6 inches across the **beam**; she displaced 46,328 tons. The vessel had three propeller screws and was powered by two 15,000-horsepower, four-cylinder triple expansion engines that each turned one shaft; a 16,000-horsepower turbine turned her center shaft. She could carry 2,603 passengers and a crew of 892. Her speed was 22 knots.

The *Titanic* left Southampton, England, on April 10, 1912, bound for New York City. On board were 1,316 passengers and a crew of 885. On April 14, while in the north Atlantic Ocean, the *Titanic* received warnings that there were icebergs in her path. However, the captain did not receive the last warning.

At 11:40 p.m., about 95 miles south of the Grand Banks of Newfoundland, Canada, the ship's lookout saw an iceberg dead ahead. The ship turned hard to the left and missed the iceberg, but a submerged ice spur ripped through 300 feet of *Titanic's* right side, puncturing six forward watertight compartments.

Once the damage was assessed, the *Titanic's* captain knew the ship would go down. He sent out a distress call, but it would take four hours for the nearest ship, the *Carpathia*, to reach the disabled vessel. To avoid panic, the passengers were not told the seriousness of the situation.

The *Titanic* was carrying more than 2,220 on board, but had enough lifeboats for only 1,178. This was partly because regulations regarding lifeboats had not been updated to match the increasing sizes of the ships being built. Even so, when the *Titanic's* lifeboats were lowered, some of them were not even filled to capacity. Many passengers wouldn't leave the vessel, refusing to believe the magnificent ship would go down.

When the *Titanic* was half submerged, there was a loud groaning sound, and the great ship broke in two. At 2:20 a.m., the *Titanic* sank, taking the lives of more than 1,500 passengers and crew. When the *Carpathia* finally arrived, she picked up 711 survivors from the *Titanic's* lifeboats.

After the *Titanic* sank, new laws were passed that required ships to carry enough lifeboats for all their passengers. In addition, liners began crossing the Atlantic in routes farther to the south, and an ocean ice patrol was instituted.

World War I (1914–1918) accelerated the development of the airplane. Aircraft were used for reconnaissance, bombing, and the roaring **dogfights** that made some pilots legends. This caused a demand that planes fly faster, climb higher, and become more maneuverable.

In the early days of aerial combat, bombs were dropped by hand and fliers shot at each other with pistols and rifles. Later, gunners accompanied pilots, but still used hand-held weapons to shoot at the enemy. Sometimes, planes would simply ram each other. On October 5, 1914, a French observer used a machine gun strapped to the nose of his plane to shoot down a German observation aircraft. He was a lucky man—if his machine gun had disabled his propellers, he would have shot himself down.

Then came a turning point. The French pilot Roland Garros modified a *Morane-Saulnier* monoplane by adding wedge-shaped, steel deflector plates to the rear of his plane's wooden propeller blades, enabling him to shoot through the propeller's arc. On April 1, 1915, Garros downed a German plane. In a period of 16 days, he shot down four more. The French people called him an "ace" (a word previously used for athletes). When an American reporter wrote about this ace and his five kills, a new term was born. Hereafter, a pilot earned the title "ace" with his fifth kill.

On April 19, 1915, Garros himself was downed by German ground fire and German officials discovered his innovation. However,

it was Anthony Fokker, a Dutch designer working for the Germans, who truly revolutionized air combat by inventing the synchronizer gear, which automatically timed a plane's machine gun to fire only when a propeller blade would not be hit.

Soon the Fokker E.I Eindecker was rolling out of German factories. This single-seat monoplane had an 80-horsepower engine, a braced mid-wing design and was equipped with Fokker's new invention. It enabled the Germans to dominate the air and soon earned the nickname the "Fokker scourge."

Hauptmann Oswald Boelcke, the ace who virtually created Germany's devastating air force, flew the first of Fokker's E-planes. Boelcke pioneered the strategy of using fighter squadrons on offensive missions and is credited with creating modern air combat. One of

The Fokker E.I

the pilots under Boelcke's command was Manfred Freiherr von Richthofen, the famous Red Baron who scored a total of 80 kills.

Eventually the British captured one of Fokker's planes and copied his invention, but from the autumn of 1915 until the spring of 1916 Germany ruled the skies. At one point the British tried to offer Fokker $10,000,000 to work for them. German intelligence intercepted the offer, and Fokker didn't learn about it until after the war was over.

German submarines were called U-boats, from the German word *unterseeboot*. To stop supplies from reaching Britain during World War I, Germany designated the waters surrounding the British Isles a War Zone. In February 1915 all-out submarine warfare was declared, and within three months 68 ships were sunk in the War Zone. The U-20 was

A typical German U-boat

one of many German submarines hunting English ships but she became one of the most famous because she was the sub that sank the *Lusitania* (see no. 44).

On April 30, 1915, the U-20 left Emden, Germany, to attack British ships off the coast of Liverpool, England. In command of its 42-man crew was Captain Walter Schweiger, a submarine veteran experienced in sinking English ships. The U-20 was cramped and hot. Fumes from its diesel engines seeped though the small ship. Caged mice were kept on board to test the air in the boat. If the fumes reached a poisonous level, the mice would die; while the mice were alive, it was safe to breathe the air.

During the first week of May 1915, U-20 was off Ireland when it sank a small schooner, the *Earl of Latham*. In accordance with the Hague Convention, the schooner's crew was allowed to abandon their ship. On May 6, the U-20 sank two more English merchant ships, *Candidate* and *Centurian*. The crews of these ships were also allowed to safely get off their boats. At this point, Schweiger realized he did not have enough fuel to go to Liverpool and return to Germany, so he decided to remain in the waters off the Irish coast.

On May 7, the U-20 was on the surface when a huge ship came steaming straight toward her. The U-20 dove, and when the oncoming ship was about a half a mile away, Schweiger fired a torpedo, striking the vessel in the forward starboard side. Shortly after the torpedo hit, there was a second, enormous explosion. As he looked through the U-20's periscope and watched the "horrible spectacle" of people trying to escape the ship, Schweiger realized he had just fired on the *Lusitania*. Already full to capacity, the U-20 could not surface to pick up survivors. Later, the radio operator said, "We were truly sorry."

Captain Schweiger claimed he fired only once. He later reported he was surprised that one torpedo caused such massive damage and wrote, "It would have been impossible for me to fire a second torpedo into this crowd of people struggling to save their lives."

When the U-20 returned to Germany, its crew was hailed as heroes. In 1917 Captain Schweiger was killed when the U-boat he was commanding was sunk by the English Navy.

Although World War I brought advances in the development of aircraft, the oceans that separated the continents still existed as huge expanses across which people simply did not fly. However, in 1919 two pilots flew an English bomber across the Atlantic ocean nonstop from Canada to Ireland.

The English engineering, arms manufacturing, and shipbuilding company, Vickers Ltd. began building aircraft in 1911. Vickers planes served in World War I, but the Vickers Vimy F.B.27, a reliable long-range bomber that first flew on December 30, 1917, did not see combat in that war. With the conflict over, Vickers began to explore ways to use the large plane to carry civilians.

The Vickers F.B.27 was a **biplane**, with a biplane tail unit and space for a three-person crew. Powered by two 360-horsepower Rolls Royce Eagle VIII engines, it was designed to carry a bomb load of 2,000 tons and was one of the biggest planes of its time.

The first nonstop air crossing of the Atlantic took place June 14–15, 1919. Two Englishmen, Captain John Alcock, a former Royal Naval Air Service pilot, and Lieutenant Arthur Whitten Brown, an ex-Royal Flying Corps observer who served as navigator for the flight, flew from St. John's, Newfoundland, Canada, to Clifden, County Galway, Ireland. For this journey, the Vickers Vimy was stripped of its combat elements and fitted with extended-range fuel tanks that carried a total of 870 gallons of fuel. Also on board were 40 gallons of oil and six gallons of water.

Alcock and Brown flew 1,890 miles at an average speed of 119 mph. Their total flying

The Vickers Vimy

time was 16 hours, 12 minutes. The open cockpit prevented conversation, and they battled clouds and fog for almost the entire trip. The Vimy's instruments were mounted outside the plane on the engine **cowlings**, and when the aviators encountered rain, snow and hail, the instruments were unreadable. Deprived of his instruments and unable to see the stars, sun or moon, Brown navigated by **dead reckoning**.

Once in Ireland, Alcock set the Vimy down in what appeared to be a lush field, only to discover after landing that it was a bog. The soft ground caused the plane to partially nose over on landing, but neither man was hurt.

The Atlantic had previously been crossed by air in May 1919 by U.S. Navy Lieutenant Commander A.C. Read, flying a Curtiss NC-4 flying boat. However, Read made stops along the way. The Vickers Vimy F.B.27 made the first nonstop flight across the Atlantic, and with it, the world became a little smaller.

51. Fokker F.II
1920

After the end of WW I, war planes were converted from military to civilian use. Some aircraft companies simply found new uses for their war planes. Many designers reworked the existing planes that had proven themselves in combat. However, the visionary designer Anthony Fokker began to build completely new aircraft.

During the final days of WW I, Fokker left Germany and returned to Holland, where he planned to establish a new factory. Other designers were clinging to the biplane configuration, but Fokker built the F.II, a new **monoplane** transport. The F.II was first built in Germany, where it was designated the V.45. The prototype took to the air in October 1919, and was flown to Holland in March 1920.

Powered by a 185-horsepower liquid-cooled engine, the F.II had a wingspan of 52 feet, 10 inches and was 38 feet, 3 inches long. It had a cantilever wood wing set on top of the body and bolted to the top of the **fuselage**. The fuselage was square, and tapered toward the rear of the plane. The wing skin was plywood, and the body and tail were assembled using fabric-covered welded steel tubes. A solid deep section gave the aircraft good strength and superior lift at low speeds. However, it increased drag at high speeds. The F.II had a maximum speed of 93 mph, but cruised at 75 mph, which was slower than the 100-mph speed of other airliners. Its **range** was 745 miles, it had a service ceiling of 13,120 feet, and was piloted by a crew of two.

One of Fokker's most important innovations in the field of early commercial air travel was an enclosed cabin for passengers. When people traveled on the remodeled military planes used by other companies, they had to climb a ladder to reach a high open cockpit and then fly exposed to the weather. The F.II's closed cabin provided seats and other "conveniences."

Fokker's F.II was the first airliner built for the Dutch carrier **KLM**, which was founded on October 17, 1919. The F.II could accommodate four passengers in the cabin, and a fifth seated next to the pilot in the open cockpit if the plane was flown by a single pilot. The new airliner flew for the first time on September 30, 1920.

One of the world's first truly successful passenger planes, the F.II was imitated, copied, and improved upon by a number of designers, and used by several early airlines. It also paved the way for a succession of high-performance airliners, including Fokker's F.VII ten-seat plane—which had a 360-horsepower engine and a cruising speed of 84 mph—and the F.VII-3m, the three-engine plane that became the 1920s most popular airliner.

The Fokker F.II

The seven airmen who flew around the world

The Douglas World Cruiser was a two-seat biplane powered by a single 420-horsepower Liberty piston engine. It was 35 feet, 6 inches long and 13 feet, 7 inches high, with a wingspan of 50 feet. It had a fuel capacity of 600 gallons. Its maximum speed was 103 mph, its cruising speed was 53 mph, and it had a range of 2,200 miles. On April 4, 1924, four Douglas World Cruisers took off from Seattle, Washington. Their goal was to fly around the world together.

Plane #1, *Seattle*, piloted by the mission's flight commander, got as far as Alaska, where it crashed into a mountain. The crew survived, and after a two-week journey over snow-covered terrain, they finally arrived at a small town.

Plane #3, *Boston*, developed engine problems when an oil pump failed over the Atlantic Ocean, and it was forced down near the Faeroe Islands between Iceland and Great Britain. While it was being hauled aboard the navy destroyer *Richmond*—one of many ships standing by— the *Richmond's* boom broke and landed on top of the plane, destroying it. The *Boston's* pilot cried at the sight. The crew

completed the trip in a replacement plane.

Planes #2, *Chicago*, and #4, *New Orleans*, completed the trip, returning on September 28, 1924, to become the first aircraft to fly around the world. The two planes made 56 stops in 29 countries; the *Chicago* and *New Orleans* flew 28,945 miles in 175 days, logging a total of 365 hours in the air. In the course of this historical voyage, 73 separate flights were made and 17 engines were used. Only three of the flights were more than 600 miles; the longest was 803 miles, from Reykjavik, Iceland, to Frederiksdal, Greenland.

Commissioned specifically by the U.S. Army for this round-the-world attempt, these planes were modified Douglas NT torpedo bombers that were equipped with **pontoons** for the first part of their journey. Once in India, with the next phase of the flight over land, the pontoons were removed and wheeled landing gear was mounted on the planes. In England, the pontoons were reinstalled for the trip home across the Atlantic.

The fliers who completed the trip returned to a hero's welcome, and the new company started by Donald Douglas, which had built the first planes to fly around the world, had proven itself. The Douglas Aircraft Company would eventually become one of the world's biggest and most important aircraft producers.

Today, the *Chicago* is on display at the National Air and Space Museum in Washington, D.C. The *New Orleans* is in the Air Force Museum in Dayton, Ohio.

Josephine Ford
1926

Admiral Robert E. Peary reached the North Pole by foot in April 1909, but almost 20 years later no one had yet flown over the top of the world. In 1926 Commander Richard Evelyn Byrd, Jr. (1888–1957), a retired U.S. Navy officer, and pilot Floyd Bennett set out do just that in the *Josephine Ford*.

Named for the daughter of Edsel Ford, one of the expedition's backers, the *Josephine Ford* was a tri-motor Fokker monoplane fitted with

The Josephine Ford

Wright Whirlwind J-4B engines. The Whirlwind was an air-cooled engine that used air from its propeller wash to cool the heat it generated. It also had sodium-filled valves to help prevent overheating.

The *Josephine Ford* arrived in Norway on April 29, 1926, on board the ship *Chantier*, which carried the plane in two pieces. The fuselage was unloaded onto a hastily-con-structed raft; then, the 63-foot wing was lowered and bolted to the fuselage.

When fitted with wheels, the *Josephine Ford* could cruise at 70 mph. When fitted with skis, which caused more air resistance, her speed was slower. After three failed take-offs—two of which broke the plane's skis—on May 9, at 12:37 a.m., the *Josephine Ford* took

off from Kings Bay, West Spitsbergen, Norway. Her instruments included a **sextant**, an **altimeter**, two **magnetic compasses**, a **sun compass** and two **chronometers**. The round-trip distance to the North Pole was 1,535 miles. Byrd expected that he and his pilot Bennett would reach their destination and return in about 22 hours.

The flight went smoothly until, an hour short of the Pole, there was an oil leak from a reserve tank in the **starboard** engine. Bennett throttled the engine down, and the plane continued to fly at 60 mph. The leak finally stopped on its own. After the flight, the aviators discovered the leak was caused when a rivet was shaken loose and lost. The leak stopped when the oil level in the reserve tank fell below the rivet hole.

The *Josephine Ford* reached the North Pole on May 9 at 9:04 a.m. Flying at 3,000 feet, she circled the top of the world for 14 minutes. Byrd later wrote that he and his pilot were "two insignificant specks of mortality flying in a small plane, speechless and deaf from the motors, just a dot in the center of 10,000 miles of visible desolation."

The *Josephine Ford* returned to Kings Bay at 4:07 p.m. that same day, and her two passengers were hailed as heroes. There was some speculation that they had not actually accomplished their goal because they returned after only 15 1/2 hours, well under Byrd's original estimate of 22 hours. Nevertheless, the *Josephine Ford* went down in history as the first airplane to fly over the North Pole.

54. Spirit of St. Louis
1927

On May 20, 1927, at 7:52 a.m., Charles A. Lindbergh (1902–1974) took off from Roosevelt Field, Long Island, New York, in his plane, the *Spirit of St. Louis*. His destination was Paris, France. When he landed at Le Bourget airport, a few miles from Paris, at 10:22 p.m. on May 21, he had completed the first nonstop solo flight across the Atlantic Ocean—and made himself an instant international hero.

The *Spirit of St. Louis* was a single-engine high-wing monoplane specially built for Lindbergh by the Ryan Company of San Diego, California. It was 27 feet, 9 inches long and 8 feet, 9 inches high, with a wingspan of 46 feet. Powered by a 237-horsepower Wright Whirlwind J-5C radial piston engine, its maximum speed was 125 mph, and this specially modified aircraft was designed to have a range of 4,210 miles.

Named in honor of the St. Louis businessmen who financed the flight, the *Spirit of St. Louis* was virtually a flying gas tank. A forward tank carried 89 gallons of fuel; three tanks located above the ceiling carried 153 gallons, and the entire cabin, as well as the area normally reserved for the pilot, were given over to an enormous 209-gallon tank. When the plane took off, it weighed 5,000 pounds, more than half of which was gasoline—about 451 gallons of fuel. This left only a tiny area behind the forward tanks for a basic cockpit that offered no forward vision. To see where he was going, Lindbergh had to put his head out the side window or use a small periscope.

To make the plane as light as possible, Lindbergh had it stripped of everything that wasn't absolutely essential. He eliminated night equipment, including running lights, fuel-tank gauges (he kept track of his fuel by using a watch and recording engine revolutions), gas tank dump valves, a **sextant**, and even a parachute. Lindbergh allowed himself only 30 pounds for survival gear, including water and food and, in case he went down over water, three flares and a 10-pound rubber boat without oars.

Because he was flying alone, Lindbergh's biggest challenge was fatigue. During the flight he did everything he could to keep himself awake, including slapping his face, using his fingers to hold his eyelids open, stamping his feet, pinching himself, and opening the window and putting his face in the ice-cold slipstream.

Lindbergh flew about 3,600 miles in 33 hours, 30 minutes and 30 seconds. He arrived in Paris to a tumultuous welcome. The *Spirit of St. Louis* became one of the most famous aircraft in history and now hangs in the National Air and Space Museum in Washington, D.C.

Lindbergh with the Spirit of St. Louis

55. Bremen
1928

A German ocean liner, the *Auguste Victoria*, signaled the beginning of the era of "floating palaces" (see no. 42). Almost four decades later, the *Bremen* was proof that Germany remained a major presence in the trans-Atlantic passenger trade.

The *Bremen* was the **flagship** of Germany's Norddeutscher-Lloyd Line. Launched on August 16, 1928, she was the biggest ocean liner in the world and became the fastest liner of the early 1930s. She displaced 51,656 tons, and was 938 feet long and 102 feet across the **beam**. Powered by 135,000-horsepower turbine engines that turned four screws, her cruising speed was 26.25 knots. She had two funnels and 11 decks; she could carry up to 2,224 passengers and a crew of 960.

The *Bremen* was the first liner to be designed with a **bulbous bow**, and her bow had a sharp **rake** below the waterline. This configuration gave the *Bremen* more speed, reduced fuel consumption, improved her buoyancy, and lessened pitching in rough seas. She was also the first liner whose **hull** had no rivets. Instead, her hull was built with iron plates that were welded together using a new metal-working technique developed during World War I. Welding the hull created a smoother, sleeker surface that contributed to

the *Bremen*'s speed. In another first, she carried a catapult-launched seaplane, something no other liner had done before.

On her maiden voyage on July 16, 1929, the *Bremen* set trans-Atlantic records in both directions reaching New York in 4 days, 14 hours and 42 minutes. In 1933, her average speed across the Atlantic was 28.51 knots, and she held the **Blue Riband** trophy until 1935. She and her sister ship *Europa* became known as "the greyhounds of the Atlantic."

The *Bremen* was berthed in New York when World War II began in September 1939. She secretly set sail a few days later. The British fleet hunted her, intent on taking her as a prize of war, but her captain managed to steer her safely to the Russian port of Murmansk. As she crossed the ocean, her crew painted her battle gray and lined her decks with drums of diesel fuel; German dictator Adolf Hitler had ordered the *Bremen* to be set on fire if she were captured.

A few weeks after arriving in Murmansk, the *Bremen* tried to reach Germany, but she was located by a British submarine. However, she again slipped away from her pursuers, arriving in Germany undamaged.

Now in the war, the *Bremen* became a German naval barracks ship and was repainted with an elaborate camouflage design. However, she was not destined to survive World War II. In 1941 she was destroyed in a fire believed to have been set by Germans opposed to Hitler.

The Bremen

Even as progress was being made in powered aviation, some people continued to believe in the superiority of balloon flight. Large balloons gracefully sailed through the air with no engine roar, carried people in large, enclosed cabins that eliminated cold and exposure, and made flying a luxurious social experience. Count Ferdinand von Zeppelin (1838–1917) was so instrumental in designing and developing self-propelled lighter-than-air crafts that his name has become synonymous with these airships. Steerable airships were also called dirigibles. One of the greatest dirigibles in history was the *Graf Zeppelin.*

The *Graf Zeppelin* was 776 feet long and carried 3,037,000 cubic feet of hydrogen stored in bags, or cells, in a semirigid balloon. Nonrigid dirigibles relied on the gasses inside the balloon to hold their shape; rigid versions had a metal frame inside the balloon to hold their shape.

Under the front end of the *Graf Zeppelin*'s balloon was a cabin designed like a railroad car. At the front was the control room and behind it was a chart and radio room. Then came the kitchen, a dining room and passenger lounge. Behind those were five luxurious staterooms, bathrooms, and space for baggage.

Suspended from the back end of the balloon were five enclosed compartments called gondolas, each with a 550-horsepower engine and a propeller. Each gondola also had a separate control station, and all five engines were coordinated from the ship's bridge. The airship's balloon contained a series of girders that maintained the dirigible's shape, and catwalks that were used by the 41-man crew to move about the ship. Ladders led down to the gondolas. The *Graf Zeppelin* carried 20 passengers.

In November 1928, Dr. Hugo Eckener—a close associate of von Zeppelin, who assumed control of the Zeppelin company after his death— piloted the *Graf Zeppelin* from Lakehurst, New Jersey, to Friedrichshafen,

The Graf Zeppelin

Germany. He covered 3,967 miles in 71 hours, 7 minutes and set a world record for straight-line distance. So the *Graf Zeppelin* was already famous when Eckener announced that he intended to fly around the world with passengers, each of whom would pay $2,500 for making the trip.

On August 8, 1929, at 12:40 a.m., thousands of people cheered as the *Graf Zeppelin* took off from Lakehurst on the first round-the-world pleasure trip by air. The ship rarely flew above 1,000 feet, and for the next several days the passengers experienced all the wonder and beauty of air travel.

After making stops in Germany, Japan and Los Angeles, the *Graf Zeppelin* returned to New York City in triumph on August 28. She had gone around the world in 21 days, 7 hours and 34 minutes, flying almost 22,000 miles. The age of commercial air travel had begun.

The first flight across the Pacific Ocean was made in 1928 by the *Southern Cross*.

A three-engine Fokker F.VIIb-3m monoplane, like the *Josephine Ford* (see no. 53), the *Southern Cross* had a less-than-glorious history. Originally named *Detroiter*, it was one of two planes purchased by the arctic explorer George Hubert Wilkins for a 1926 expedition over the Arctic Ocean. At the dedication of the planes, a reporter backed into one of the *Detroiter's* spinning propellers and was decapitated. During the expedition, the *Detroiter* suffered engine failure and went down.

In 1927 two Australians, Captain Charles Kingsford-Smith and Charles Ulm, received money from an Australian politician to fly from the United States to Australia. They bought Wilkins's *Detroiter*, which now had no engines, fitted it with three Wright Whirlwinds, and rechristened it the *Southern Cross*, after the constellation seen in the Southern Hemisphere. They later lost their financial backing, but American businessman G. Allan Hancock bought the plane and let them use it.

The *Southern Cross* had a wingspan of 71 feet, 3 inches and was 47 feet, 7 inches long. Her cruising speed was 111 mph. Kingsford-Smith loaded the aircraft with radios and navigational instruments that included three steering compasses and two **drift meters**. When two Americans, Harry Lyon and James Warner, signed on as navigator and radio

The Southern Cross

operator, they were ready to take on the Pacific.

At dawn on May 31, 1928, the *Southern Cross* took off from Oakland, California. The four men had little room in the small cockpit. The only way they could communicate over the roar of the engines was by hand signals and scrawled notes. After some 26 hours in the air, they landed on the Hawaiian island of Oahu.

The next day they set out on the longest leg of the trip—3,200 miles from Hawaii to Fiji. After 33 hours, during which the plane was buffeted by tropical storms and a clogged fuel line almost shut down one of the engines, the *Southern Cross* arrived at the island of Suva, becoming the first plane to land in the Fiji Islands.

Two days later they made the final leg of their trip. The *Southern Cross* was tossed about the sky for hours as it battled storms so fierce that it took both Kingsford-Smith and Ulm to control the plane. But at 10:50 a.m. on June 9th, they landed in Eagle Farm, Brisbane, Australia, where thousands of people were waiting. The four aviators were joyously paraded through the city.

They had covered 7,400 miles in 83 hours, 15 minutes flying time, setting a new world record. In acknowledgment of this achievement, G. Allan Hancock gave Kingsford-Smith and Ulm the *Southern Cross*.

Richard Evelyn Byrd, Jr. was not only the first person to fly over the North Pole (see no. 53), but the first to fly over the South Pole as well. He accomplished this second feat on November 28–29, 1929 in a Ford Tri-Motor **monoplane**, the *Floyd Bennett*.

Byrd christened his plane for the veteran aviator who was his pilot on the North Pole expedition, *Floyd Bennett*, who died of pneumonia in 1928. The *Floyd Bennett* was an all-metal, cantilever high-wing monoplane with a 525-horsepower Wright Cyclone engine in the nose and a Whirlwind 220 under each wing.

The distance from Byrd's starting point of Little America in Antarctica to the South Pole was 875 miles one way. With a total of 965 horsepower, the *Floyd Bennett* consumed gas so quickly that she could not make the 1,750-mile round trip without refueling. To solve this problem, before the flight, some 350 gallons of fuel in 70 5-gallon cans were stored about 450 miles south of Little America to refuel the plane after she crossed over the Pole.

On November 28, 1929, with the Norwegian pilot Lieutenant Bernt Balchen at the controls, Byrd as navigator, and a radioman and aerial photographer aboard, the *Floyd Bennett* took off for the bottom of the world. To communicate over the roar of the engines, they strung a wire through the plane, from the cockpit back to the navigator's compartment. A wheel with a harness

was attached to the wire. When they needed to communicate, they wrote a note, attached it to the harness, and ran it back on the wheel.

The trip went well except for one potentially fatal incident. Approaching Liv Glacier at an altitude of 8,200 feet, the *Floyd Bennett* could fly no higher because it still carried most of its fuel. However, at that altitude it was still 1,300 feet beneath the glacier's full height. Balchen ordered a 150-lb. bag of food jettisoned, but the plane still could not clear the glacier. Another bag of food was thrown out, but a downward air current from the glacier kept the plane from rising. Balchen then gambled on the possibility that within the downdraft there might be a back current that would take them up. He flew the aircraft right up to the glacier, so close that its right wing nearly made contact with the ice; the *Floyd Bennett* gained the lift it needed, clearing the glacier by 200 feet.

At 1:14 a.m., South Pole time, the men on the *Floyd Bennett* sent this message announcing they had reached their destination: "The airplane is in good shape, crew all well. . . . We can see an almost limitless polar plateau."

The Floyd Bennett

The Winnie Mae

In 1929, the dirigible *Graf Zeppelin* set the record for traveling round-the-world (see no. 56). However, Wiley Post, a pilot from Oklahoma, wanted to "take the record away from the balloons." Post and an Australian navigator, Harold Gatty, readied a plane for such a trip.

The aircraft was a specially-equipped, cantilever high-winged monoplane Lockheed Vega 5B with a single Pratt & Whitney Wasp engine. The plane had a streamlined **fuselage** made with two half-shells of plywood, pressure-formed to shape through the use of a concrete mold. Post named the plane after the daughter of his financial backer, oilman F. C. Hall. The *Winnie Mae* would go on to capture two round-the-world records.

On June 23, 1931, at 4:56 a.m., the *Winnie Mae* set out from Roosevelt Field, Long Island, New York. Over the next eight days, she made 11 stops, including Blagoveshchensk, Russia, where she was mired in mud for 14 hours, and Edmonton, Canada, where they encountered mud again, forcing Post to take off from a concrete highway next

to the airfield. On July 1, at 8:47 p.m., the *Winnie Mae* returned to Roosevelt Field, having flown 15,596 miles in 8 days, 15 hours and 51 minutes. It was a new world record.

Two years later, Post set out in the *Winnie Mae* to become the first person to fly around the world solo. On July 15, 1933, he took off from Floyd Bennett Field, in Brooklyn, New York. A fierce storm plagued him for much of the flight. Post later attributed his success to his "copilot"—the Sperry Pilot automatic pilot. This was the first autopilot system, and was not yet in production, but Post had persuaded Sperry to let him use the prototype. At one point, Post flew blind for seven hours, completely dependent on the automatic pilot. Post returned to Floyd Bennett Field on July 22, having flown 7 days, 18 hours and 49 minutes, and established his second world record.

On his historic flight Post had help from other new developments in aviation. The **Automatic Direction Finder** (ADF) allowed him to use radio stations to determine his position. In addition, the **variable pitch propeller** increased the efficiency of the engine and overall performance of the plane.

The *Winnie Mae* made history again in March 1935. Post added a **supercharger** and, dressed in the first pressure suit, which he designed, flew from California to Cleveland, Ohio, riding the jet stream.

Later that year, Post went on a pleasure tour of Alaska and Siberia with his friend, humorist Will Rogers. On August 15, 1935, they were killed when their plane—not the *Winnie Mae*—crashed during a takeoff in Alaska.

The first passenger liner to exceed 1,000 feet in length, the *Normandie* was the largest and fastest trans-Atlantic ship of the mid-1930s.

A French vessel, she was launched at St. Nazaire, France, on October 29, 1932. With a gross tonnage of 83,432, a length of 1,029 feet, a width of 118 feet, 11 decks, and three huge smokestacks, she was considered the greatest ship in the world. The *Normandie* was so big that the harbor at Le Havre, France, had to be deepened for her passage. When she traveled between Le Havre and New York the press called her "the new wonder of the world."

The *Normandie* was a beautiful liner that could carry 1,972 passengers and had a crew of 1,345. Designed as a floating museum that showcased French culture, she was elaborately decorated with paintings and sculpture. She even had a 380-seat movie theater.

She was efficient as well as beautiful. Her turbo-electric engines were the most powerful engines in the world. She had four propeller screws, her boilers consumed 1,200 tons of oil a day, and her cruising speed was more than 29 knots.

The *Normandie* made her maiden voyage in May 1935 and crossed the Atlantic in four days, three hours and two minutes. She captured the **Blue Riband** trophy, and streamed into New York proudly flying a 40-foot long blue pennant.

No liner had done this before. In 1937 the vessel was refitted with four-bladed screws, and she crossed the Atlantic in three days, twenty-two hours and seven minutes, at an average speed of 31.2 knots—beating her own previous record.

The *Normandie*'s design elements included a clipper **bow** and an extremely tall **hull** that was full in its midsection and tapered toward the bow and **stern.** This hull design enabled her to sail at high speeds and maintain these speeds with great fuel economy.

After Germany conquered France in 1940, the Germans claimed her as a prize of war. However, at the time she was safely docked in New York. When the United States entered World War II in December 1941, the *Normandie* was taken over by the U.S. Maritime Commission, renamed the *Lafayette*, and converted to serve as a troop transport.

Sadly, this great ship came to an untimely end. On February 9, 1942, a spark from a welder's torch set a shipment of life jackets ablaze on board the ship. The fire spread rapidly and consumed the vessel, which capsized in her berth. It took two years to raise the *Normandie*; she was eventually scrapped in 1946.

The Normandie

One of the most famous ships of all time—and for 15 years the fastest trans-Atlantic ocean liner—the *Queen Mary*, along with her sister ship the *Queen Elizabeth* (see no. 66), were the ultimate "floating palaces." These great vessels have also come to mark the end of an era: they were among the last of the great liners to regularly ply the Atlantic before air travel became the preferred way to cross.

The *Queen Mary* was built by John Brown and Company at Clydebank, Scotland. Launched on September 26, 1934, she displaced 81,237 tons, was 1,019 feet long and 119 feet wide. She had a passenger capacity of 2,139 and could carry a crew of 1,101. Her 162,176-horsepower turbines drove four screw propellers that gave her a cruising speed of 28.5 knots. She had a clipper **bow**, 151 watertight compartments, ten anchors, and her rudder weighed 140 tons. Regarded as a symbol of England's recovery from the

the next two years she and the *Normandie* (see no. 60) alternated as the holder of the **Blue Riband** trophy until, in 1938, the *Queen Mary* claimed the all-around fastest Atlantic crossing with a time of 3 days, 20 hours and 42 minutes. The *Queen Mary* kept the Blue Riband until after World War II, when she lost it to the last great liner, the *United States*.

Like the *Normandie*, the *Queen Mary* was in New York when World War II began. In 1940 she sailed to Sydney, Australia, where she was converted to a troop ship. She once carried a record number of 16,683 passengers, the largest number of soldiers ever transported on one voyage. In addition to troops, she also carried British Prime Minister Winston Churchill and the British chiefs of staff three times.

In 1946 the *Queen Mary* served in another capacity when, as part of "Operation Baby Carriage," she brought hundreds of thousands of war brides and their children from England to the United States.

The Queen Mary

On July 1, 1947, the *Queen Mary*, now refitted and equipped

Depression, the *Queen Mary* was decorated with wood from every country in the British Empire.

Her maiden voyage, from Southampton, England, to New York, began on June 1, 1936. She arrived in New York in 4 days, 27 minutes. Later that year, she improved her time to 3 days, 23 hours and 57 minutes. For

with radar, became a luxury passenger liner again. Her last voyage began on October 31, 1967, after which she was taken out of service and sold to an American company.

The *Queen Mary* is permanently berthed at Long Beach, California, where she is open to the public as a hotel and museum.

The Douglas DC-3 has been called the world's most successful airliner; some have called it the most significant commercial plane ever built.

In 1930, a newly formed company called Transcontinental and Western Air (TWA) asked the Douglas Aircraft Company to design a 12-passenger plane that could fly at 145 mph. Douglas's chief engineer, Arthur E. Raymond, was given the job. The first thing he did was to fly coast-to-coast on the plane TWA was then using most often, a Ford Tri-Motor. On the flight, Raymond had to shout to talk to the person across the aisle, his feet "nearly froze," and the plane vibrated so much "it shook the eye glasses right off your nose." After enduring this miserable flight, Raymond knew exactly what kind of airplane he wanted to build.

The DC-1 (Douglas Commercial) first flew on July 1, 1933, and it ushered in the age of modern commercial flight. An all-metal, cantilever aircraft with a low-wing con-figuration, the DC-1 had a 710-horsepower Wright Cyclone engine under each wing, **variable-pitch propellers**, split wing flaps to increase lift, hydraulic brakes, and a stream-lined design. Its large, comfortable passenger cabin was soundproofed better than any plane before it, and featured foot rests and individual reading lights. The DC-1 was a prototype and never entered commercial service. Instead, TWA used it as a promotional tool. It set a record for a coast-to-coast flight of 13 hours, 4 minutes, and established 18 other

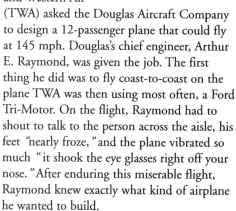

The DC-3

speed and distance records.

The slightly revised DC-2 followed. Flying for the first time on May 11, 1934, this 14-passenger plane had a speed of 190 mph and was embraced by airlines around the world.

Then came the DC-3, which first flew on December 17, 1935, and carried 21 passengers. Powered by two 1,000-horsepower Pratt & Whitney engines, the DC-3 had a speed of 195 mph and a range of 1,480 miles. American Airlines was the first carrier to fly the DC-3, beginning service on June 7, 1936. The first European carrier to fly it was KLM in 1936. By 1939 the DC-3 was flying 90 percent of the world's airline passengers.

An extremely dependable aircraft, the DC-3 developed an astounding safety record. At a time when few planes survived 1,000 hours air time, many DC-3s logged more than 60,000 hours. Its basic design was still in service as late as 1991.

The DC-3 also saw military service, as a modified version designated the C-47; the British called the aircraft the Dakota. These planes took part in the D-Day invasion during World War II, the Berlin Airlift (1948–1949), the Korean War, and, as the AC-47D, in the Vietnam War.

The Focke-Wulf Fw 61

The first documented design for an aircraft that could fly straight up using rotating parts rather than floating up as a balloon, was created by Leonardo da Vinci in 1500. His design was based on an "air screw," a rotating wing that "screwed" the craft into the air. In 1842 W. H. Phillips built an unmanned steam-driven machine with rotating blades that was propelled by small jets at the tips of the blades. In 1903 Thomas Edison made a model helicopter powered by an electric motor, but it failed to get off the ground. A person first went aloft in free flight by helicopter in 1907, when Paul Cornu flew a twin-rotor craft near Lisieux, France. However, it wasn't until June 26th, 1936, that the first entirely successful helicopter flight took place.

That flight was made by the Focke-Wulf Fw 61, a single-seat, twin-rotor helicopter designed by Professor Heinrich Karl Johann Focke during 1932–34. It had a nose-mounted 160-horsepower engine that provided power to two three-bladed rotors spinning in opposite directions. The nose engine also powered a small propeller that helped cool the engine. The rotors were placed above the **fuselage**, attached and supported by tubes, and driven by a shaft that ran up one of the tubes. Vertical control was achieved by using the throttle to vary the number of rotor revolutions.

On its maiden flight, the Focke-Wulf Fw 61 stayed in the air for an official time of 28 seconds, although Focke's log book indicated 45 seconds. While many other designers had been experimenting with helicopter designs and rotorcraft, the Focke-Wulf Fw 61 was the breakthrough that demonstrated the helicopter was a practical flying machine worth pursuing and developing.

In June 1937, the Fw 61 set a helicopter endurance record by staying in the air for 1 hour, 20 minutes and 49 seconds. It also established helicopter world records for altitude at 8,000 feet, speed of 76.15 mph, straight-line distance of 10.19 miles and closed-circuit distance of 50.09 miles. In 1938, the renowned German test pilot Hanna Reitsch flew the Fw 61 in a demonstration of helicopter flying in Berlin.

Though it was quite successful, the Focke-Wulf Fw 61 was not put into commercial use. However, Reitsch's demonstration led the German airline Deutsche Lufthansa to order a passenger version of the Fw 61. During 1940, the Focke-Achgelis Fa 223, which was developed to fill the order, became the first helicopter to be put into full, though limited, production.

64. Hindenburg
1936

The sister ship of the *Graf Zeppelin* dirigible (see no. 56), the *Hindenburg* was designed to be the perfect trans-Atlantic airship. In its time, it was the world's largest dirigible.

The German Zeppelin company began work on the huge ship in the fall of 1931. Its **hull** was 803.8 feet long, 30 feet longer than the *Graf Zeppelin*, and it had a diameter of 135.1 feet. The *Hindenburg* also had large fins that were almost 100 feet long, 50 feet wide and 11 feet thick at the root. The lower fin contained a secondary steering station that could operate the ship if the main controls failed.

Inside the hull, steel girders formed 16 compartments for the gas cells. Along the bottom of the ship, on both sides of the **keel**, were the freight rooms, crew quarters, water tanks, and fuel oil. Toward the front of the dirigible was the control car.

Passenger accommodations were on two decks inside the hull and included large, elaborate cabins for 50 people. The upper deck measured 49 feet by 92 feet and had a dining room, a lounge, and a writing room. The lower deck contained a smoking room and the kitchen.

Four engine gondolas, placed two by two, hung below the middle and rear of the ship. The *Hindenburg* was powered by four 1320-horsepower Daimler-Benz 16-cylinder diesel engines.

To eliminate the danger of the gas catching fire, Dr. Hugo Eckener—the ship's chief designer—planned to use helium in the *Hindenburg*. Helium provided less lift than hydrogen, but was nonflammable. However, large quantities of helium had to be obtained in the United States, and America had stopped allowing the exportation of helium at that time. Because helium was unavailable,

hydrogen was used instead.

When the *Hindenburg* made her maiden voyage on March 4, 1936, she had not yet been officially named. She first flew as the *Hindenburg* on March 31, 1936, carrying 37 passengers to Rio de Janiero, Brazil. In 1936, Eckener also received a permit to make ten trips from Germany to Lakehurst, New Jersey. The *Hindenburg* soon became an extremely popular ship.

On May 6, 1937, the *Hindenburg* was set to arrive at Lakehurst with 97 people aboard

The Hindenburg in flames

when she burst into flames and crashed, killing 36 people (22 crew members, 13 passengers and 1 ground crewman). The spectacular destruction of the *Hindenburg*—captured on film and on live radio—is one of the most famous disasters in aviation history. The cause of the fire was a mystery. Some theories say it was an accident; others suggest it was destroyed by sabotage. Whatever the cause, the *Hindenburg's* fiery death signaled the end of dirigibles as commercial passenger carriers.

Franklin Delano Roosevelt (1882–1945) guided the United States through the Depression and World War II. The *Potomac*, the presidential yacht from 1936 to 1944, was one of his favorite places to relax.

Originally named *Electra*, the *Potomac* was a U. S. Coast Guard cutter, a steam vessel used for coastal, ice, and weather patrols. Completed on October 26, 1934, the *Electra* was a 165-foot vessel weighing 376 tons, with a cruising speed of 10–13 knots.

At this time, the presidential yacht was the 100-foot *Sequoia*, but Roosevelt was not happy with this boat. She was decorated with rich wood, and Roosevelt thought she was too fancy. In addition, because Roosevelt was confined to a wheelchair, he had to be carried around the *Sequoia*, which he hated. His staff also worried because so much of the ship was flammable. Roosevelt asked the navy to look for a different ship, and they chose the *Electra*.

On January 30, 1936, the *Electra*, renamed the *Potomac*, was moved into the shipyard at Norfolk, Virginia, and refitted. On March 2, 1936, she was officially commissioned and placed into service.

One of the new features of the vessel was an elevator installed in a false smokestack. Roosevelt insisted on an elevator he could operate himself using a rope and pulley; this way he would not only be able to get around the boat on his own, but exercise, too.

Roosevelt was very pleased with the *Potomac*. On board this ship he entertained the King and Queen of England, held press conferences, worked on war plans, and once addressed the nation from her radio room.

After Roosevelt died, the *Potomac* was transferred to the State of Maryland, where she became a fisheries research vessel and occasionally the governor's yacht. Later, she

The Potomac

was sold to private owners and used as a transport in the West Indies. In 1964, the vessel was bought by the singer Elvis Presley, who donated her to a fund-raising effort for St. Jude's Hospital in Memphis, Tennessee.

She was resold often. In 1980, San Francisco authorities seized her on suspicion that she was being used by drug smugglers. She was taken to Treasure Island in San Francisco Bay, where she sank when a floating piling penetrated her hull. She was raised by members of the Navy Reserve and, in 1981, was bought at auction by the Port of Oakland, California. In 1990 she was designated a National Historic Landmark.

The *Potomac* was restored to her presidential glory, and in 1995 was put on public display in Oakland. She also became a floating classroom where students could learn about the Great Depression and World War II.

The sister ship of the *Queen Mary* (see no. 61), the *Queen Elizabeth* was the largest passenger ship ever built. Displacing 83,673 tons, she was 1,031 feet long— about 11 feet longer than her sister—and 119 feet across the **beam**. Her four turbines generated 181,700 horsepower and turned four screws, giving her a cruising speed of 28.5 knots. She was designed to carry 2,288 passengers and a crew of 1,296.

Constructed at John Brown's shipyard in Scotland, the *Queen Elizabeth* was planned as a luxury ship, but with World War II looming, she was secretly equipped for battle. Launched in September 1938, she quietly left Southampton, England, for New York in February 1940, five months after the war in Europe broke out. She was painted battle gray, and her portholes were painted black, so she would be a hard target to see for enemy planes and ships. Although the German air force, the Luftwaffe, dispatched bombers with orders to sink her on sight, she raced across the Atlantic on a zigzag course, evading U-boats, bombers, and German ships. The *Queen Elizabeth* arrived safely on March 7th, docking next to the *Queen Mary* and the *Normandie* (see no. 60).

In November she sailed to Singapore, where she was converted to a troop ship with a capacity for 8,200 soldiers. By the end of the war, she and the *Queen Mary* had carried a total of 1,243,538 soldiers. These vessels were so important to the war effort that Adolf Hitler offered a bounty of $250,000 for either ship's destruction. Fortunately, their speed enabled them to elude German U-boats.

After the war, the *Queen Elizabeth* worked as part of "Operation Baby Carriage," in which she carried thousands of war brides and their children from England to the United States. She then returned to commercial passenger service, making her first such trip on October 16, 1946.

Withdrawn from passenger service in 1969, she was bought by a group of Americans. Berthed at Port Everglades, Florida, she became a tourist attraction, floating hotel, and convention center. She was later sold to a Hong Kong businessman and, in February 1971, sailed to her new home in Hong Kong, where she was to be turned into a floating university.

She never began her fifth career. On January 9, 1972, she caught fire in what was believed to be an act of sabotage. It took so much water to put out the fire that the huge liner was structurally damaged. The next day, she capsized. The *Queen Elizabeth* could not be salvaged, and she was ultimately scrapped.

The Queen Elizabeth

Some aviation historians have called the Spitfire the best-known British aircraft of World War II. If not for this plane, the Royal Air Force (RAF) might not have been able to save England from the attacks of the German Luftwaffe in the Battle of Britain in 1940.

In 1935 there were no modern monoplanes in the RAF. Plans to strengthen

The Spitfire Mk V-B

England's air force focused on the biplane. The Spitfire started out as an all-metal, cantilever low-wing monoplane powered by a 600-horsepower Rolls Royce Goshawk II Vee engine. It was designed by a team led by Reginald Mitchell to meet RAF specifications. However, the plane disappointed both the government and its designer, so Mitchell started again with his own ideas.

The result was a new, sleeker and smaller single-seat fighter. Equipped with retractable landing gear, it had the new Rolls Royce P.V. 12 Merlin engine and elliptical wings carrying eight machine guns that fired outside the propeller disc. This time, the Air Ministry created its specifications around the aircraft. The prototype, which had a 900-horsepower Rolls Royce Merlin 'C' engine, took to the air on March 5, 1936. It proved to be excellent in handling and overall performance, and the plane was ordered into production. However, by September 1938, with the threat of war

with Germany growing, only five Spitfire Mk Is were in service. When war was declared one year later, on September 3, 1939, the RAF had nine combat-ready Spitfire squadrons.

When the Battle of Britain began on August 8, 1940, the RAF had 19 squadrons of Spitfire Mk Is (1,400 aircraft), and 32 squadrons of Hurricanes (2,309 aircraft), 2,100 of which could be sent aloft each day. German air strength on the Western front was more than 6,500 fighters and bombers, more than half of which were thrown against England. Every time the Spitfires took to the air, they were vastly outnumbered. England's survival is testimony to both her pilots and the planes they flew.

Like Germany's Messerschmitt (see no. 69), the Spitfire was customized to meet different needs. Variations included clipped wings for low-altitude flying, increased wingspans for higher altitudes, and different weapon configurations. Choices for weaponry included two cannons and four machine-guns; four cannons; or two cannons, two 12.7-mm machine guns, and up to 1,000 pounds of bombs.

The Spitfire was in production for the entire war, and a total of 20,335 were built. It was used not only by England but by her allies as well, including the United States and Russia.

This dependable plane was also used after the war. The last Spitfire mission was flown by a photo-reconnaissance Mk 19, on April 1, 1954, in Malaya (Malaysia today), in southeast Asia.

The Lockheed 10 Electra was a major development in transport planes for the Lockheed Aircraft Company. An all-metal, cantilever low-wing monoplane with a tail that had twin fins and rudders, it was powered by two Pratt and Whitney Wasp Junior SB engines and could carry ten passengers. The prototype was flown on February 23, 1934, and it entered regular air service later that year. By the late 1930s, Electras were flown by eight U.S. airlines and other airlines around the world.

The Electra will forever be a part of history because the Electra 10-E was the plane in which Amelia Earhart (1897–1937), the most famous American woman aviator of all time, disappeared.

The Electra 10-E was similar to the first Electra (10-A) but had two 600-horsepower Wasp S3H1 engines. Only 15 10-Es were built; Earhart's plane bore the registration number NR16020. Earhart had her ten-passenger aircraft modified, adding fuel tanks to the wings and fuselage. This gave her plane a fuel capacity increased from 250 to 1,000 gallons to achieve a theoretical **range** of 4,000 miles.

In 1928, Earhart made the first trans-Atlantic flight by a woman when she flew as copilot in the Fokker F.VII *Friendship*. She became a national heroine, even though she later said the pilot didn't allow her to touch the controls. In 1932, Earhart made the first solo trans-Atlantic flight by a woman when she flew from Harbour Grace, Newfoundland, to Londenderry, Northern Ireland. Three years later she made the first solo flight by a woman from Honolulu, Hawaii, to the American mainland at Oakland, California.

In 1937, Amelia Earhart set out to become the first woman to fly around the world. Deciding not to embark alone, she chose to fly with Fred Noonan, a veteran navigator. They took off from Miami, Florida, on June 2, 1937 and planned to return on July 4th.

By June 30, they reached New Guinea. Two days later they took off for Howland Island, a tiny speck in the Pacific, 2,556 miles away. The next morning, the U.S. Navy cutter *Itasca*, which was in the water near Howland Island to act as a radio beacon, received messages from the Electra that reported Earhart and Noonan were lost. They were also low on fuel and could not determine their position by radio bearings. Earhart and Noonan disappeared on July 2, 1937. Neither they nor their aircraft were ever found, and the disappearance remains one of aviation's great mysteries.

Amelia Earhart once described how she felt about flying when she said, "The love of flying is the love of beauty. It was more beautiful up there than anything I had known."

Amelia Earhart with her plane

A captured Me 262 A-1

The Treaty of Versailles, which ended Word War I, forbade Germany to rearm. Nevertheless, during the 1930s Germany created a vast aircraft industry, and along with it the most powerful air force in Europe—the Luftwaffe.

The Messerschmitt Bf 109 was the potent mainstay of the Luftwaffe during World War II. It was designed by Willy Messerschmitt in 1934. The **stressed-skin** monoplane with a small enclosed cockpit had wings half as big as similar planes. The smaller wings gave the plane more speed, and a major innovation—automatic slats along the wing's front edge—provided greater lift at lower speeds and during close maneuvering. The Bf 109 was so unconventional that the WW I German ace General Udet declared, "That will never make a fighter!" Less than a year later, Udet called it the best fighter in the world.

In a 1937 international flying competition, the Messerschmitt won a speed event and a climb/dive event. Several months later, a Bf 109 with a specially-enhanced engine set a new world landplane speed record of 379 mph. The plane first saw combat in the summer of 1937 during the Spanish Civil War, where it proved vastly superior to whatever flew against it. By the time WW II began, Germany had more than 1,000 of these versatile new fighters in service.

The Bf 109 was used throughout WW II. More than 35,000 were built, and they were produced in many different versions. The major production version was the Bf 109G. Powered by one 1,800-horsepower Daimler-Benz DB 605AM inverted V-12 piston engine, it had a maximum speed of 386 mph, a range of 447 miles, and a service ceiling of 38,550 feet. It was flown by a single pilot, and armed with two 13-mm machine guns and three 20-mm cannon.

The Messerschmitt Me 262A-1a was the first **turbojet** aircraft to enter service with any air force, becoming operational on October 3, 1944. A twin turbojet **swept-wing** fighter, it carried four 30-mm Mk 108 cannons in its nose and often had 12 55-mm rocket missiles under each wing. The rockets, which were aimed using a standard gunsight and electrically fired at about 650 yards from the target, proved extremely effective against bomber formations. Another Messerschmitt variation, the Me 262A-2a, was fitted with two bombs beneath the nose and was one of the first jet bombers in operational service.

There were delays in getting the Me 262A-1a into full service because of problems building reliable engines with enough thrust. Had this plane entered the war earlier, it might have significantly aided the German cause because it would have made Allied daylight bombing of Germany too dangerous.

There have been eight U.S. Navy ships with the name *Enterprise*. The most famous is the seventh—the aircraft carrier affectionately called the "Big E".

Commissioned on May 12, 1938, the *Enterprise* was the second of three Yorktown-class carriers (along with the *Yorktown* and the *Hornet*) constructed just before World War II. She displaced 25,500 tons, measured 809 feet, 6 inches long and 83 feet, 2 inches **abeam**, and her flight deck was 802 feet long. In 1943 she was refit to be a little longer and wider, and be better able to withstand torpedo hits.

Powered by turbine-driven quadruple screws, she had a top speed of 32.5 knots. She carried eight 5-inch guns, 16 antiaircraft guns, and 24 Browning machine guns. (After 1943, she also mounted 40 Bofors radar-directed antiaircraft guns and 50 additional antiaircraft weapons.) She operated 96 aircraft, and her full wartime personnel numbered 2,919.

During 1942, the *Enterprise* saw action at Guadalcanal, the Solomon Islands, Wake Island, and the Battle of Midway. Fought in June 1942, Midway was a watershed event in naval combat. The engagement began with an attempted Japanese invasion of Midway Island in the Pacific. American planes based at Midway attacked the Japanese fleet while it was some 600 miles out at sea. The next day, planes from four Japanese carriers bombed American forces on Midway.

Planes from the U.S. carriers *Enterprise, Yorktown,* and *Hornet* attacked the Japanese carriers, sinking four of them in two days. Japan also lost most of her experienced carrier-based pilots; the heavy losses forced the Japanese to retreat. Midway was the turning point in the Pacific sea war; in its aftermath, Japan never regained military dominance in the Pacific. Midway was also the first naval battle fought at the range of carrier-based planes instead of at the range of ships' guns.

During the battle, the *Yorktown* was sunk and the *Hornet* was set ablaze. With both ships out of action, the *Enterprise* was the last operational U.S. carrier in the Pacific. She fought alone until she was joined by the *Saratoga* in early December 1942, and a sign on her hangar deck read *"Enterprise* vs. Japan."

During the war, the *Enterprise* took her share of attacks. She was hit three times by Japanese kamikaze bombers. She became the most decorated U.S. ship of WW II, with 20 **battle stars**.

Decommissioned in February 1947, she was docked at Bayonne, New Jersey. The Navy decided it would be too expensive to modernize her for the faster, heavier planes then in use, and after three attempts to preserve her as a memorial failed, she was sold for scrap on July 1, 1958.

The current *Enterprise* is the world's first nuclear-powered aircraft carrier.

The launch of the "Big E", October 1936

71. Admiral Graf Spee
1939

The Treaty of Versailles, which ended World War I in 1918, limited the size of German battleships to 10,000 tons. However, between 1930 and 1940 the German navy side-stepped this restriction by building three large, powerful cruisers—ships used for reconnaissance, reporting enemy activity during battle, and protecting trade. These three ships were called pocket-battleships, because they were better armed and armored than the typical cruiser, yet smaller than the typical battleship. The most famous of the three was the *Admiral Graf Spee*, also called the *Graf Spee*.

Launched on June 30, 1934, the *Admiral Graf Spee* was 610 feet long, 67 feet 7, inches across the **beam** and displaced 11,900 tons. Her 56,800-horsepower diesel engines were highly efficient and economical, giving her a

The Graf Spee on fire

top speed of 28 knots and a range of 12,500 miles at 13 knots. She was armed with six 11-inch guns mounted in two triple turrets, eight 5.9-inch guns, and 18 anti-aircraft guns. She was protected by armor that was 3 inches thick at the waterline, as much as 5.5 inches thick on her turrets, and 1.5 inches thick on her deck.

In September 1939, the *Graf Spee*, commanded by Hans Langsdorff, began sinking ships in the South Atlantic. By December she had claimed nine kills, and British squadrons were searching for her. Commodore Henry Harwood, commanding the English cruiser *Ajax*, correctly guessed where the *Graf Spee* was hunting. He had two other English cruisers, the *Exeter* and *Achilles*, meet him off the east coast of South America, near the River Plate, on December 12.

The next day, the *Graf Spee* appeared. She engaged the *Exeter, Ajax,* and *Achilles* in the first naval battle of World War II, the Battle of the River Plate. Better armed and more heavily armored than the three British cruisers, she inflicted so much damage on the *Exeter* that the cruiser retreated after 25 minutes. Then the *Graf Spee's* big guns damaged the *Ajax*, and she too withdrew. The *Graf Spee* was only slightly damaged and could have pursued the retreating ships, but instead sailed into the port of Montevideo, Uruguay, at the mouth of the River Plate. The *Ajax* and *Achilles* followed.

The German vessel was given permission to stay in Montevideo for four days to make repairs. During this time, the Germans were fooled into believing that a large British force was waiting for the *Graf Spee* outside the port.

The Germans were determined to prevent the capture of their ship by this "greater" force. On the night of December 17, Langsdorff took his ship out to sea. When he reached international waters at the three-mile limit he **scuttled** the vessel. Three days later, Langsdorff took his own life.

Regarded as the most famous Japanese single-seat fighter plane of all time, the Mitsubishi Zero-Sen was built to specifications designed by the Imperial Japanese Navy.

The Zero was a cantilever low-wing, single-engine monoplane. The A6M1 prototype flew for the first time on April 1,

Japanese Zeros preparing to take off to bomb Pearl Harbor

1939. Carrying the standard Zero armament of two 7.7-mm machine guns in the fuselage and two 20-mm cannons in its wings, the A6M1 was powered by a 780-horsepower Mitsubishi MK2 Zuisei engine. It performed well, but did not meet the required speed of 310 mph, so the A6M2 was built next as an improved model.

The A6M2 was powered by a 925-horsepower Nakajima NK1C Sakae engine, and took to the air on January 18, 1940. The first A6M2s were the Navy Type O Carrier Fighter Model 11. This plane was soon followed by the Model 21, which had manually-folded wingtips and offered improved maneuverability. The A6M2 had a wingspan of 39 feet, 4.5 inches and was 29 feet, 9 inches long. Its maximum speed was 316 mph and it had a **range** of 1,165 miles. This new plane was so impressive that in July, 1940 15 pre-production models were ordered for duty in Japan's war against China, and the Zero was ordered into full production.

During World War II, the Zero served Japan as the Messerschmitt (see no. 69) served Germany and the Spitfire (see no. 67) served Great Britain. Throughout the war it was the foundation of Japanese air power, and was

produced in many different versions designed for a variety of missions and tasks.

The Zero first saw combat as a fighter and fighter-bomber over China. It was an instant success. The Allies assigned it the code name "Zeke," and from 1941, until the Battle of Midway in June 1942, it dominated the Pacific skies.

The Zero was in operational service for all of World War II. Three companies, Mitsubishi, Nakajima, and Hitachi, built a total of 10,965 planes. Wave after wave of Zeroes bombed Pearl Harbor in 1941. The final version, the A6M6c, which went into production late in 1944, carried two 20-mm cannons in its wings, three 13.2-mm machine-guns (two in the wings, one in the **fuselage**), and underwing rails for launching eight 22-lb. or two 132-lb. air-to-air rockets.

Late in the war, with the tide turning against Japan, Zeroes made up the first officially-formed *kamikaze* unit. This unit—*kamikaze* translates as "divine wind" in Japanese—sent planes loaded with 250-kg. bombs on suicide missions to deliberately crash into Allied ships. In 1945, Mitsubishi produced 465 A6M7s, a Zero designed specifically for *kamikaze* missions.

The Arizona after the attack at Pearl Harbor

The battleship *Arizona* will forever be linked with the Japanese attack on Pearl Harbor, which brought the United States into World War II.

Work on the *Arizona* began on March 16, 1914, at the New York Naval Shipyard in Brooklyn, New York. She was launched on June 19, 1915, and christened with a bottle of the first water to spill over Roosevelt Dam as well as the traditional champagne. The *Arizona* was commissioned on October 17, 1916. She displaced 31,400 tons, was 608 feet long, 97 feet, 1 inch across the **beam**, and had a speed of 21 knots.

During World War I, she served as a gunnery training ship. The *Arizona's* oil-burning engines prevented her from seeing combat as part of the British Grand Fleet, because England had more coal than oil. In November 1918, she was part of the honor escort that brought President Woodrow Wilson to the Paris Peace Conference.

From 1929–1931, the *Arizona* was modernized with new boilers and new turbines, and fitted with more horizontal armor for protection from air attack. Afterward, she carried President Herbert Hoover on a vacation cruise through the Caribbean.

On December 7, 1941, the *Arizona* lay at anchor with other U.S. ships along "battleship row" in Pearl Harbor, Hawaii. At 7:55 a.m., Japanese planes attacked. At 8:10 a.m., the *Arizona* was hit by a 1,760-pound armor-piercing bomb. Seconds later, the forward powder magazines exploded, destroying the front part of the ship and igniting intense fires. The *Arizona* sank in less than nine minutes, taking 1,177 sailors and marines down with her.

By the time the attack on Pearl Harbor ended, eight ships were sunk or beached and 2,403 lives were lost. Fortunately, the U.S. fleet's aircraft carriers, which were at sea on maneuvers when the attack occurred, were spared.

Before the attack, Americans were divided about entering World War II. However, news of the destruction at Pearl Harbor unified the country. In the words of Japanese Admiral Isoruku Yamamoto, who had planned the attack but was personally opposed to war with the United States, the attack on Pearl Harbor "awakened a sleeping giant and filled him with a terrible resolve."

On December 1, 1942, the *Arizona* was removed from the registry of U.S. Navy vessels. She was never raised, and today is a national monument at Pearl Harbor in Honolulu. A 184-foot long concrete structure has been built across the sunken ship. Visitors are ferried out to this structure, which consists of a large open area where people can observe the submerged battleship, and a smaller area designed as a shrine, where the names of those killed on the *Arizona* have been inscribed in marble.

74. B-17 Flying Fortress
1941

In May 1934, the U.S. Army sent out a call for an advanced bomber plane that could carry a bomb load of 2,000 pounds a distance of at least 1,020 miles—and ideally as far as 2,200 miles—at a speed of 200–250 mph. The plane was to be used primarily for long-distance bombing runs on ships at sea.

The Boeing company's response was the Boeing Model 299, which first flew on July 28, 1935. Three weeks later, the new aircraft, powered by four 750-horsepower Pratt & Whitney Hornet engines, impressed military authorities when it flew nonstop a total of 2,100 miles to its official test ground at an average speed of 252 mph. With this combination of speed and endurance, military aviation entered a new era.

Subsequently designated the Y1B-17, this new bomber was a cantilever monoplane with a low-wing design and huge wings so thick that at their root they were half the diameter of the **fuselage**. The wings were fitted with wide-span **trailing-edge** flaps for taking off and landing at lower speeds. The Y1B-17 was armed with five machine guns and carried a bomb load of 4,800 pounds.

The B-17 Flying Fortress

The first B-17s took to the air on December 2, 1936, powered by four 930-horsepower Wright Cyclone radial engines and piloted by a crew of nine. In 1938 further refinement equipped the B-17 with 1,000-horsepower engines enhanced with a Moss/General Electric turbocharger, which used an exhaust-driven turbine to maintain the pressure of the air entering the engine. (Maintaining air pressure is especially important at high altitudes, where the air gets thinner.) From that point on, turbocharged engines were standard on all B-17s. Later models also increased the number of machine guns from five to seven.

The B-17C was flown by England's Royal Air Force before the United States entered World War II. Designated Fortress I, she first saw combat in a high-altitude attack over Wilhelmshaven, Germany, on July 8, 1941. It was thought that flying high would protect the huge bombers from attack, but Messerschmitt fighters (see no. 69) could reach them at altitudes as high as 32,000 feet. In addition, the B-17 was particularly vulnerable to attack when approached head-on.

The B-17E was given the large fin and rudder that became standard on all later Fortresses. The B-17E also introduced the tail gun turret. To counter the threat from frontal attack, the B-17G added a "chin" turret under the nose that carried two 12.7-mm machine guns.

The B-17, in its various configurations, was used extensively by the U.S. Eighth Air Force in its daylight bombing raids over Germany from 1943-1945. By the end of the war, some 13,000 B-17s had been built.

75. B-24 Liberator
1941

A formation of B-24 Liberators

The next step forward in building long-range bombers after the B-17 (see no. 74), was the B-24. There were more B-24s than B-17s built, and the B-24 became the most widely produced U.S. aircraft in World War II. It also saw combat in more theaters of operation for a longer period of time than any other heavy bomber.

When the B-24 was being planned by the Consolidated Aircraft Corporation, the U.S. Army wanted a long-range bomber that would out-perform the B-17. Consolidated equipped its new bomber with four wing-mounted 1,200-horsepower Pratt & Whitney Twin Wasp engines. The wing was mounted in a shoulder configuration to provide greater **fuselage** capacity. Wide-span **trailing-edge** flaps helped give the bomber adequate handling at low speeds and allowed for a suitable landing speed. The bomb bay could handle up to 8,000 pounds and had new "roller shutter" doors that slid back into the fuselage, reducing drag. The bomb bay was divided in two by the fuselage **keel** beam, which was used as a catwalk by the crew to get from one end of the plane to the other.

The Royal Air Force ordered 164 of the new bombers, designated YB-24, and gave them the name Liberator. The first six planes reached Britain in March 1941 and were used as unarmed transports.

The Liberator was the first RAF aircraft that was capable of bridging what was called the Atlantic Gap, the expanse of ocean in which ships were outside the range of U.S. or British planes. The next group of B-24s the RAF received was used to provide air support for ships.

The B-24 first saw operational use as a bomber in June 1942 in the Middle East. This LB-30 model had power-operated turrets, each with four 7.7-mm machine guns, in the mid-upper and rear of the fuselage, and was flown by a crew of ten. One LB-30, the *Commando*, was British Prime Minister Winston Churchill's personal transport.

The B-24 Liberators joined the B-17 Flying Fortresses in the U.S. Eighth Air Force's devastating daylight bombing raids against Germany. Many of these airborne battleships were decorated with colorful, imaginative "nose art" painted by the men who flew them. On these daylight raids, up to 1,000 B-24s and B-17s took to the air at a time. Accompanied by fighter escorts, they flew hundreds of miles into German territory to damage and destroy factories and weapons sites.

In addition to its invaluable service in Europe, the B-24 was used to great effect in the Pacific war, where its long range made it especially successful. In all, more than 19,000 Liberators were built.

76. Bismarck
1941

Named after one of the most famous 19th century German statesman, the *Bismarck* was one of Germany's prize battleships at the outset of World War II. Soon after she took to sea, she became the target of an intensive hunt by the British Navy. The determined effort to sink this mighty warship became one of the most famous naval engagements of the war.

Construction on the *Bismarck* began in 1935. She was launched in February 1939 and was completed in her berth, in the begin-

The Bismarck

ning of 1941. Displacing 50,900 tons, she was 823 feet long and 118 feet across the **beam**. Powered by three powerful turbines that turned three screws, she could make 30 knots and had a range of 8,100 miles at 19 knots. She mounted eight 15-inch guns and numerous anti-aircraft guns. Her **hull** and deck armor ranged from 1.5 inches to 12.6 inches, the armor protecting her **conning tower** was up to 14 inches thick, and the armor on her gun turrets varied from 1.7 inches to 14 inches. She carried a crew of more than 2,000 men. This powerful ship was

built in deliberate violation of the 1918 Treaty of Versailles, which limited the size of German battleships to 10,000 tons.

On May 18, 1941, accompanied by the heavy cruiser *Prinz Eugen*, the *Bismarck* sailed from Gdynia, Poland, its mission to attack English convoys in the North Atlantic. However, her departure was discovered, and she was pursued by British ships. On May 24, the *Bismarck* engaged England's largest warship, the battle-cruiser *Hood*, and a new battleship, *Prince of Wales*. The *Bismarck* sank the *Hood* and damaged *Prince of Wales*, but was hit three times during the battle. One of these hits caused her to lose the use of 1,000 tons of fuel oil. Later that day, the *Bismarck* was hit by a torpedo from planes launched from the carrier *Victorious*, but suffered no damage.

On May 25th, the loss of fuel caused the *Bismarck* to make for port on the French coast, pursued by more than 40 British ships. The British ships lost track of her, but on the morning of May 26 they reestablished contact and followed her all day. That night, planes from the carrier *Ark Royal* launched torpedo attacks and the *Bismarck* was hit three times. Only the third torpedo did serious damage, striking her rudders and leaving her incapable of steering. She was attacked throughout the rest of the night and hit by five more torpedoes.

On the morning of May 27, the destroyers *King George V* and the *Rodney* began firing on the *Bismarck* with heavy guns. In less than an hour she was completely disabled. The *Bismarck* was ultimately sunk by torpedoes fired by the cruiser *Dorsetshire*.

77. Jeremiah O'Brien
1941

During World War II, it was crucial for the Allied war effort to maintain the stream of war supplies flowing to Europe and the Pacific. In response to this need, U.S. shipyards mass-produced merchant vessels that came to be known as Liberty ships. By 1945, a total of 2,770 Liberty ships had been constructed.

All-welded hulled ships, with an average displacement of 10,500 tons and a general speed of 11 knots, they were based on a design that had been developed in 1879 in Newcastle, England. Simple, efficient vessels that could be built quickly, they were easy to operate, had capacity to carry big cargoes, and could keep functioning even after suffering considerable damage. They were exactly what the Allies needed to keep the war effort going. Of all the Liberty ships built, two have been fully restored and are still in operation. One of them is the *Jeremiah O'Brien*.

Built in 56 days in South Portland, Maine, the *Jeremiah O'Brien* was launched on June 19, 1943. Displacing 14,245 tons, she is 441 feet, 6 inches long, 57 feet **abeam** and powered by a 2,500-horsepower three-cylinder, triple expansion steam engine.

The *Jeremiah O'Brien*'s first year of operation included four trips as part of a convoy between the United States and England. Immediately after the D-Day invasion on June 6, 1944, she served as a shuttle ship between Britain and the Omaha and Utah beachheads in Normandy, making 11 trips to support Allied forces.

After the war, the *Jeremiah O'Brien* carried war brides from Australia to the United States. In February 1946, she and hundreds of other merchant ships became part of a reserve fleet based near San Francisco, California. Many of these ships were decommissioned and went into commercial service throughout the United States. Some were sold to other countries, and some were scrapped or deliberately sunk to become artificial reefs.

In the 1960s, it was decided that a Liberty ship should be saved and preserved for historical purposes. In 1978, the *Jeremiah O'Brien*, which was still in very good condition, was chosen. Fully restored, she became active again in 1979. Her first annual cruise took place on May 21, 1980.

On April 18, 1994, a volunteer crew took her to Normandy to participate in the ceremony marking the 50th Anniversary of D-Day. On June 6, 1994, the *Jeremiah O'Brien* lay off Pointe du Hoc, the only one of 6,000 ships in the original invasion to return to Normandy for the ceremony. On this voyage she also made 14 port calls, and returned to the United States on September 23, 1995. Following this trip she was put on public display in San Francisco, Calfornia.

The Jeremiah O'Brien, 1944

84

The Pacific theater of operation during World War II was a huge expanse of tiny islands and open water. To wage war over such a vast area, a big bomber with great range was necessary.

While preparing for war in Europe, U.S. military officials spoke of a VHB (very heavy bomber). For the war in the Pacific, they used the designation VLR (very long range). When the army sent out its call for VLR designs in 1940, the Boeing company responded with what would become the B-29 Superfortress. The prototype, designated Model 345, flew on September 21, 1942.

To meet military specifications Boeing designed a cantilever **monoplane** with a wing mid-set on the **fuselage**. This wing design would result in a high landing speed, so Boeing included wide-span **trailing-edge** flaps that increased the wing area by about 20 per cent and permitted landings at lower speeds. The new bomber was powered by four Wright Cyclone twin-row radial engines, each with two General Electric turbochargers. It had a cruising speed of 230 mph, a maximum speed of 358 mph, and a range of 3,250 miles. The B-29 could fly farther and carry the biggest bomb load of any plane yet built.

Weighing more than double the original Flying Fortress (see no. 74), the B-29 had a new design that included pressurized crew compartments. This allowed the crew to stay in the air for ten hours, at altitudes exceeding 30,000 feet. It had five remote-controlled, power-operated gun turrets, which were connected to the crew compartments with crawl-

The Enola Gay returns after dropping the atomic bomb

tunnels. For armament, it carried either two 12.7-mm machine guns in each turret and three 12.7-mm machine guns, or two 12.7-mm machine guns and one 20-mm cannon, in the tail turret.

Almost 4,000 B-29s were produced. In addition to flying combat missions during the war, the B-29 also contributed to research and experiments in supersonic flight after the war, launching the rocket-powered aircraft that were attempting to break the sound barrier.

The most famous B-29 of all is the *Enola Gay*, the plane that dropped the atomic bomb on Hiroshima, Japan, on August 6, 1945. The *Enola Gay* was one of 15 B-29s that were specially modified for atomic bomb missions. They were equipped with new propellers, new engines, and pneumatic bomb bay doors that opened and closed faster than the standard ones. The *Enola Gay* was named in honor of the mother of mission commander Colonel Paul Tibbets; he had the name painted on the plane just before the *Enola Gay* took off.

Today, parts of the *Enola Gay* are on display at the National Air and Space Museum in Washington, D.C.

The Missouri

The *Missouri* is the last of four U.S. battleships in the Iowa class, which were large, fast American battleships averaging 48,000 tons. The others were the *Iowa*, *New Jersey*, and *Wisconsin*. With the exception of the Japanese ships *Yamato* and *Musashi*, these vessels are the largest, most powerful battleships ever constructed. The *Missouri* is the second battleship, and fourth boat, to bear this name and is the last battleship built by the United States.

Designated BB-63 (battleship number 63), the *Missouri*'s **keel** was laid down on January 6, 1941 at the New York Naval Shipyard in Brooklyn, New York. She was launched on January 29, 1944, commissioned on June 11, 1944, and became operational on December 14, 1944.

Displacing 45,000 tons—58,000 tons when fully loaded—the *Missouri* is 887 feet long and 108 feet across the **beam**. Powered by turbines that develop a total of 212,000 horsepower to turn four propeller shafts, she has a top speed of 33 knots. She has two rudders, two five-bladed propellers, and two four-bladed propellers. Her thickest **hull** armor is 13.5 inches, the armor on her **conning tower** is 17.3 inches thick, her second deck armor is 6 inches thick, and her turret armor is 7.25-17 inches thick. Her tank capacities enable her to carry 2.5 million gallons of fuel oil, 30,000 gallons of aviation fuel, and 39,000 gallons of fresh water. Mounting nine 16-inch guns in triple turrets, she can fire a 2,700-lb. shell as far as 23 miles with daunting accuracy. During World War II, she carried a crew of 2,534.

The *Missouri* saw action in the final year of World War II, participating in the battles of Iwo Jima and Okinawa. However, she will always be remembered as the ship on which representatives of Japan officially surrendered on September 2, 1945, ending the war.

The *Missouri* also served in the Korean War, taking part in several shore bombardments. In 1955 she was decommissioned and mothballed at Puget Sound Naval Shipyard, in Bremerton, Washington.

She was recommissioned on May 10, 1986, and on her second tour of service she carried a crew of 1,515 navy personnel and 53 Marines. The *Missouri* served in the Persian Gulf War in 1991 and was decommissioned again on March 31, 1992. She was moored in Bremerton, Washington, for six years.

In June 1998, the *Missouri* steamed across the Pacific to a new home at Pearl Harbor, Honolulu, Hawaii. She was permanently berthed near the *Arizona* (see no. 73) and began a new career as a memorial and museum. The Battleship *Missouri* Memorial officially opened in 1999.

An X-1 rocket-powered aircraft named the *Glamorous Glennis* was the first plane to hit Mach 1, breaking the sound barrier.

The Mach is a unit of speed named after the Austrian scientist Ernst Mach (1838–1916), that expresses the relationship between an aircraft's speed and the speed of sound in a given place. When an aircraft reaches the same speed as the speed of sound, it has reached Mach 1. The speed of sound is not constant—it changes with temperature and altitude. At sea level, the speed of sound is about 760 mph; at 35,000 feet, it is 660 mph.

A highly experimental plane designed by the Bell Aircraft Corporation, the X-1 was a streamlined orange-and-white plane with a tiny one-man cockpit. It was 30 feet, 11 inches long and configured with very short wings and a needle-tipped nose.

The X-1 was powered by a Reaction Motor Inc. XLR-II four-chamber, 6,000-lb.-thrust, rear-mounted rocket engine that burned a mixture of liquid oxygen and alcohol as fuel. At full power, the XLR-II could fire for a maximum of 100 seconds. The rocket engines of the late 1940s could not be **throttled**. A pilot could adjust the aircraft's speed only in 1,500-pound increments.

Because of this limitation, the X-1 could not take off by itself. It had to be carried aloft by another airplane and launched while in the air. The B-29 Superfortress (see no. 78) was the only plane that could accomplish this, and in order to do it, its design had to be modi-

fied by removing its bomb bay and reshaping the lower part of its fuselage. After being dropped by the B-29, the X-1 would go into free fall until it was far enough from the B-29 for the pilot to fire the rocket engine. The X-1 was equipped with retractable landing gear so it could land by itself.

On October 14, 1947, 24 year-old veteran pilot Chuck Yeager took control of the X-1

Chuck Yeager with the Glamorous Glennis

and flew the plane into history. Ascending to 37,000 feet, the B-29 released the X-1, which had been named *Glamorous Glennis* after Yeager's wife, over California's Mojave Desert. Yeager ignited the rocket chambers one by one and roared to Mach .96, at which point his plane began to rattle and buck ferociously. Then, as the *Glamorous Glennis* achieved Mach 1, the indicator on the machmeter leapt off the scale. Flying at more than 700 mph, 43,000 feet above the Mojave, the *Glamorous Glennis* became the first plane to crash through the "brick wall in the sky" known as the sound barrier.

The *Glamorous Glennis* is on display at the National Air and Space Museum in Washington, D.C.

81. Hughes H-4 Hercules (The Spruce Goose) 1947

One of the most famous post-World War II aircraft made only one flight. Its critics didn't think it would even get off the ground.

The Hughes H-4 Hercules is the world's largest seaplane and the plane with the greatest wingspan ever built. Originally envisioned as a flying freighter that would carry troops and cargo to the Pacific theater of operation, it is a huge wooden aircraft that was nicknamed the Spruce Goose.

In August 1942, industrialist and pilot Howard Hughes (1905-1976) was approached by shipping tycoon Henry Kaiser to build the oversize plane. The project was designated HK-1, after the initials of both men. Later, Kaiser withdrew from the project and the plane was redesignated the H-4 Hercules.

Hughes's government contract specified three planes over a two-year period. Because of the war, Hughes had to use "nonessential" materials, so he built his plane with birch plywood (not spruce). Instead of rivets, which were also needed for the war, waterproof glues held the plane together. The 140-ton aircraft had a wing span of 320 feet, and its overall length was 218 feet, 6 inches. Its **hull** was 25 feet wide and 30 feet high. The Hercules was so big that a new building had to be constructed to hold it.

Powered by eight 3,000-horsepower, 28-cylinder Pratt & Whitney engines, the H-4 had a maximum speed of 218 mph, a cruising speed of 175 mph, and a range of 3,500 miles. It held 14,000 gallons of fuel in 14 separate tanks. Passages were built through the wings so engineers could inspect and repair its

The Spruce Goose

engines—in flight.

In 1944 the U.S. Department of Defense canceled Hughes's contract because the H-4 was behind schedule. However, Hughes was told to continue building one plane for test flights. Hughes completed the plane using his own money, but the war ended before the H-4 was finished. In 1947 Hughes was questioned by Congress, and one senator called the H-4 "a flying lumberyard" that would never get off the ground.

On November 2, 1947, at Long Beach Harbor, California, with Hughes at the controls, the Spruce Goose reached an altitude of 70 feet during a one-mile test flight. By then Hughes was no longer interested in manufacturing the H-4. He made the test flight only to prove that his giant plane would stay in the air. After its one flight, Hughes retired the aircraft and later gave it to the Aero Club of Southern California.

For many years the Spruce Goose was on display in Long Beach, next to the Queen Mary (see no. 61). In 1992, it was bought by Evergreen International Aviation, which transported the aircraft to McMinnville, Oregon for display at a new aviation center and museum there.

82. Kon-Tiki
1947

One of the most famous trips across the Pacific Ocean occurred in 1947 when Norwegian scientist and explorer Thor Heyerdahl (b. 1914) and five companions used a 45-foot raft named *Kon-Tiki* to sail more than 4,000 miles from South America to the Polynesian islands.

Thor Heyerdahl was a scientist who specialized in the early movements and civilizations of island-dwelling people such as the Polynesians. He believed that ancient people were capable of making great ocean voyages in primitive craft. He believed that the remote Pacifc islands of Polynesia were first settled by South American native peoples who emigrated there. Since ships were not in use in the Pacific in those times, Heyerdahl believed that if his theory were true, these early ocean voyagers must have drifted across the Pacific on rafts. In 1947, he set out to prove his theory by making the exact same voyage himself, on the same kind of raft the people of those times would have used.

First, Heyerdahl and five volunteers trekked into the remote Ecuadorian jungle to find balsa trees that were the same size as those used to make ancient rafts. They picked nine trees and floated them down a river to the Pacific coast.

In the Peruvian town of Callao, they built a raft 45 feet long and 18 feet wide, by lashing the balsa logs together with strips of hemp rope. Attached to the **stern** end of the center log was a large piece of balsa wood in which wooden pegs were set to hold a rudder. The raft had two short hardwood masts standing next to each other, and was rigged with one square sail. A small thatched-roof open bamboo hut provided shelter and a place to sleep. Heyerdahl named his raft *Kon-Tiki*, for the sun king worshipped by the Incas.

On April 28, 1947, Heyerdahl and his five companions left Callao to drift and sail across the Pacific. On August 7, after 101 days on the open water, the *Kon-Tiki* reached Raroia Reef, in the Tuamotos Islands.

However, the surf was treacherous, and the final moments of the journey turned into a battle for survival as the *Kon-Tiki* was savagely tossed about by the ocean. Those aboard finally made it to shore safely, but everything on the deck was lost. Yet the raft itself survived intact, and two weeks later the *Kon-Tiki* was towed to Tahiti by the French schooner *Tamara*. It had traveled 4,300 miles across the ocean.

The Kon-Tiki

Heyerdahl's theory was proven right — it was possible for people who possessed only the simplest type of watercraft to travel across the Pacific Ocean.

After its voyage, the Kon-Tiki was placed on display in the Kon-Tiki Museum, in Oslo, Norway.

In the years following World War II, jet propulsion became the standard engine force for warplanes. In the Soviet Union, the design bureau Mikoyan and Gurevich incorporated British Rolls Royce **turbojet** engines, one of the best engines in the world at the time, and German swept-wing design to produce what has been called "one of the most significant aircraft in history"—the Mig-15.

The Mig-15 was a cantilever, mid-wing monoplane with a 35 degree wing sweep and a tail that was mounted at the tip of its fin. Sent aloft on July 2, 1947, it was the first fully-swept piloted air-craft to take to the air. Powered by one 5,952-pound-thrust turbojet engine, it flew at 668 mph at sea level and had a range of 1,156 miles. A single-seat fighter, it was armed with one 37-mm cannon and two 23-mm cannons, and carried up to 1,102 lbs. of **ord-nance** under its wings.

Mig-15

Although its large-caliber machine cannons were of World War II design, the Mig was a formidable fighter that caught Western Allied pilots by surprise when they first encountered it fighting the Communist Chinese and North Koreans during the Korean War. American airmen who faced these planes found the Mig could fly 100 mph faster than they could. Later in the Korean War, when U.S. pilots flew more advanced F-86 Sabres, they found the Mig was still able to fly faster and higher, climb at greater speeds, and make tighter turns than the Sabres. However, the Allies had the advantages of better trained airmen and more advanced equipment, and the Migs had significant problems. They sometimes broke apart while executing extremely demanding maneuvers, and high-speed turns tended to send the planes spinning out of control.

In 1952 the Mig-17 was introduced. This newer, faster Mig was designed to eliminate the problems discovered in the Mig-15 during the Korean War. The Mig-17 had a 45 degree wing sweep, a longer **fuse-lage** that reduced drag, and a better cockpit design. A later version—the Mig-17PFU—was armed with four air-to-air guided missiles and was the first Soviet missile-armed interceptor to see combat. The Mig-17 was used extensively by North Vietnam during the Vietnam War.

In 1953, the Mig-19, a completely redesigned supersonic fighter, was introduced. It was a sleeker, bigger Mig, powered by two 7,275-pound-thrust turbojet engines. Later versions had all-weather radar (Mig-19PF) and air-to-air missiles (Mig-19PM).

The Mig-15, 17, and 19 are the most-widely produced jet fighters in history.

84. B-52 Stratofortress
1952

After World War II came the Cold War, the ongoing battle for power and strategic advantage waged between the Soviet Union and the United States. Both sides prepared for an attack. If war did come, it might see the use of atomic bombs. As part of its defense, the United States established the Strategic Air Command. SAC based its tactics on a radar network that would warn of an attack; constantly-airborne bombers would then retaliate immediately. The heart of SAC's readiness strategy was the B-52 bomber.

The Boeing company approached the U.S. Air Force with a design for an enormous turbojet long-range bomber as early as 1948, but Pratt & Whitney could not provide the necessary engine until 1952. The result was the J57, an extremely advanced power plant and the first all-American designed and built jet engine. It had two compressors that turned separate turbines to deliver 10,000 pounds of thrust, double the thrust of most earlier engines. The B-52 was so huge that it needed eight of them.

The B-52 prototype first flew on April 15, 1952. It had thin, shoulder-mounted wings and was operated by two pilots seated one behind the other. This new plane was called a Stratofortress because it flew at an altitude of 50,000 feet, and the stratosphere begins at 31,680 feet. Improvements in later models included an antiradiation under-surface finish, an enhanced control system for the rear weapons—four 12.7-mm machine guns—and advanced weapons and navigation systems.

When the first SAC squadron received the B-52 in 1956, SAC's striking power and range virtually doubled. Once the B-52 was in the air, it was refueled by KC-135 tankers. Also powered by the new J57 engine, the KC-135 could refuel planes at greater heights and speeds than previous tankers.

Later Stratofortresses, such as the B-52G, carried eight tons of onboard electronic equipment and electronic countermeasures (ECM) decoys that could be released if the plane were attacked. The decoy was a small jet plane called the Quail that had a radar signature like the B-52's, and so confused an enemy missile's radar.

B-52 Stratofortress

The final version of the Stratofortress, the B-52H, is powered by eight 17,000-pound-thrust Pratt & Whitney turbofan engines. The B-52H has a maximum speed of 595 mph, a cruising speed of 509 mph and a range of 10,000 miles. A six-seat, long-range strategic bomber, it is armed with one remote-controlled 20-mm cannon in its tail turret. It also has Skybolt ballistic missiles beneath its wings and carries Quail decoys.

In addition to serving with SAC, the B-52 saw duty as a heavy bomber during the Vietnam War, and was used to launch cruise missiles in the Desert Storm campaign in 1991.

85. Boeing 707
1954

Boeing 707

In the early 1950s, the Boeing Company began to think of the turbine jet engine, which had served bombers and fighters so well in WW II, as a power plant for a civilian aircraft. When this idea failed to arouse military or commercial interest, Boeing risked $16 million to build the prototype for an aircraft no one seemed to want. Keeping its project a closely-guarded secret, the company designated the plane Model 367-80. Employees nicknamed it the "Dash-80." Hoping for support from the military, Boeing designed the "Dash-80" as a high-speed military transport or in-flight refueling tanker.

Unveiled on May 14, 1954, the "Dash-80" was 128 feet long, with a wingspan of 130 feet. Powered by four 9,500-lb.-thrust Pratt & Whitney JT3P **turbojet** engines, it cruised at 550 mph, had a range of 3,530 miles, and a service ceiling of 43,000 feet. To showcase its value as an in-flight fueling tanker, it was equipped with a refueling boom specially developed for easy fuel transfer. Boeing's financial gamble paid off. The military ordered 29 tanker/transports, and ultimately more than 800 would be built.

With its new design a success, Boeing refitted the "Dash-80" as the civilian aircraft 707-120 that became the world's biggest, most

powerful, and smoothest-flying airliner. Pan American Airways ordered six of the planes, and when they entered coast-to-coast service in August 1958, they revolutionized commercial airline travel.

On October 10, 1959, Boeing's 707-320 Intercontinental series, which had a longer **fuselage**, more powerful engines, and greater fuel capacity than the first 707s, began flying Pan-American's New York-London route. Within a few years, all the major airlines were flying jets.

The prototype "Dash-80" never entered commercial or military service. However, it went on to have an illustrious career of its own. An airborne laboratory for 18 years, the "Dash-80" was used to test new engine-thrust reversers, engine sound suppressers, radar, and radar antennas. For a time it was flown with a fifth engine on the rear of the fuselage, and flown with three different types of engines at the same time. To test landing gear, it was outfitted with oversized tires for touchdowns and takeoffs on fields so muddy they could barely support the weight of a car. By the time it was retired in 1972, the venerable "Dash-80" had logged almost 3,000 hours in the air.

In May 1972, the "Dash-80" was given to the National Air and Space Museum in Washington, D.C. In May 1990, it was returned to Boeing to be restored, and placed on display at Boeing Field in Seattle, Washington.

The *Forrestal* was the first aircraft carrier built after World War II and was the first carrier designed to operate jets.

Launched on December 11, 1954, the *Forrestal* was the first in a new class of "super" carriers that includes the *Saratoga*, *Independence*, and *Ranger*. Displacing 80,000 tons, she is 1,039 feet long and 129 feet across the **beam**. Her heavily-armored flight deck is 252 feet wide.

While the *Forrestal* was being designed, she was reconfigured to include an angled flight deck. A British design element, the angled flight deck allowed a carrier to deploy its planes faster, and when the angle was wide enough, planes could take off and land at the same time. This design became standard on all future carriers. The *Forrestal* was also the first U.S. carrier equipped with steam catapults—she has four—for launching planes, a feature that also became standard on future carriers. In addition, she had a new type of enclosed **bow** that provided added stability on the open seas.

Her four turbine engines generate 260,000-horsepower to turn four propeller screws with five blades each, and her top speed is 33 knots. She has two rudders that each weigh 45 tons and two anchors that weigh 30 tons each.

The *Forrestal* operates more than 80 aircraft and has four aircraft elevators. Her crew, including air wing personnel, totals 5,000.

The *Forrestal* is virtually a floating city. On board are more than 950 telephones, 95 radio receivers, 75 radio transmitters and 600 closed circuit TV sets. Her sick bay has a capacity for 60 beds. It takes 300,000 gallons of paint to cover the ship and 50 gallons of paint a day to maintain her.

In the fall of 1956 the *Forrestal* served in the Mediterranean during the Suez crisis. In 1963, a KC-130F refueling tanker made 21 full-stop landings and takeoffs from her decks, becoming the largest and heaviest aircraft to land on a U.S. Navy carrier. The *Forrestal* served in the Vietnam War, and on July 4, 1976, President Gerald Ford stood on her flight deck to review more than 40 "tall ships" from around the world and officially began the U.S. bicentennial celebration.

From January 1983 to May 20, 1985, the *Forrestal* was given a $550 million upgrade. She completed her final deployment on December 23, 1991, and was redesignated as a training carrier on February 5, 1992. For the next six months she helped train new navy pilots, then sailed to the Philadelphia Naval Shipyard for another refit.

Decommissioned on September 30, 1993 and removed from the navy register, the *Forrestal* was then berthed in Philadelphia.

The Forrestal

The Nautilus

The name *Nautilus* is famous in both fiction and history. The fictional *Nautilus* was the submarine in Jules Verne's famous sea adventure, *20,000 Leagues Under the Sea*. The historical *Nautilus* is the world's first nuclear-powered submarine.

Construction of the *Nautilus* began on June 14, 1952. She first took to sea under nuclear power on January 17, 1954, and was commissioned for service on September 30, 1954. Named for the early submarine built in 1801 by Robert Fulton—as well as for Verne's fictional vessel—the *Nautilus* displaces 3,530 tons on the surface and 4,040 tons when submerged. She is 324 feet long, 28 feet across the **beam** and powered by two 15,000-horsepower steam turbines. Her nuclear reactor generates the heat that produces the steam for these turbines. She has an underwater speed of more than 20 knots and can dive to a depth of 720 feet. The *Nautilus* carries a crew of 10 officers and 95 enlisted personnel. She has six torpedo tubes.

In August 1958, the *Nautilus* became the first ship to travel from the Pacific Ocean to the Atlantic Ocean beneath the polar ice cap. In 1931 a submarine that was also named the *Nautilus* tried to make this voyage but failed. The nuclear-powered *Nautilus* reached the North Pole at 11:15 p.m. on August 3, becoming the first vessel to reach the very top of the world.

One of the reasons the *Nautilus* succeeded was that she was equipped with an inertial navigation system. Ship's Inertial Navigation System (SINS) was developed after World War II for use by nuclear subs, to enable them to navigate while remaining submerged for long periods without having to rise to periscope depth for a fix on their position. SINS works by plotting a submarine's position at the start of a voyage, then precisely measuring all increases and decreases in speed, in all directions. By comparing these figures to the vessel's original position, calculations can be made that provide a fix on its position at any point. This enables a sub commander to always know exactly where the ship is. Using inertial navigation systems, submarines have traveled completely around the world underwater.

Inertial navigation is very expensive and is used almost exclusively on nuclear submarines, though a few surface ships have it. Studies are in progress to develop simpler, less expensive inertial navigation systems.

With the development and construction of more advanced nuclear submarines, by the end of the 20th century the *Nautilus* was nearin the end of her active days; eventually she will be preserved as a memorial at Annapolis, Maryland.

Until the mid-1950s, the most common and preferred way for passengers to travel between the United States and Europe was by ship. Rather than fly, it was much more civilized—and much more fun—to make the trip on the huge "floating palaces" that glided across the Atlantic with passengers' every comfort in mind. However, all that changed on December 19, 1957, when a Bristol Britannia 312 aircraft flew from London to New York in less than a day.

After WW II, the British Overseas Airways Corporation (BOAC) put out a request for a medium-range passenger plane. Bristol and four other British manufacturers submitted eight different designs. BOAC decided that the Bristol Type 175, which could carry up to 36 passengers, came closest to what it was looking for.

Changes to the Type 175 design resulted in an airliner that could carry 90 passengers, and the Britannia 102 entered service on Feb. 1, 1957, flying BOAC's South African routes.

However, even before the Britannia 102 flew, there was already a demand for larger aircraft. Bristol responded with the Series 300, which was longer, could carry up to 133 passengers, and had the range to cross the Atlantic nonstop. BOAC ordered Bristol's Series 300LR (long-range) airliner, which became the Series 310. The prototype Britannia 311 flew for the first time on December 31, 1956. Modifications led to the Britannia 312, and regular London-to-New York service began on December 19, 1957, when the Britannia 312 made its first flight.

The Britannia 312 was 124 feet long and had a wingspan of 142 feet. Powered by four 4,120-horsepower Bristol Proteus 755 **turbo-prop engines**, it had a maximum speed of 397 mph, a cruising speed of 375 mph, and a service ceiling of 24,000 feet. Its range with maximum **payload** was 4,268 miles. A dependable aircraft nicknamed the "Whispering Giant," the Britannia 312 was kept in trans-Atlantic service by BOAC until the advent of pure jets (jet aircraft that do not have propellers).

A trans-Atlantic sea voyage was an exercise in genteel leisure, but required five days. Planes, on the other hand, could make the crossing in hours. (The Britannia 312 made the return trip from New York to London in 8 hours 48 minutes.) As airliners got bigger, more comfortable, and safer, they became the preferred way to travel.

The first trans-Atlantic pure jet service was inaugurated by BOAC on October 4, 1958, when two de Havilland Comet 4s flew simultaneously between New York and London. As crossing the Atlantic became even faster and quieter, in the mind of the public the only way to travel across the ocean was by air.

Bristol Britannia

While the United States and the Soviet Union never engaged in air combat during the Cold War, both countries did use air power to monitor each other's military activities. During the 1950s, the Eisenhower administration was intent on keeping track of any Soviet military advances, particularly in the area of atomic weapons. This policy led to the development of "spy" planes—and produced a controversial incident involving a U.S. plane called the U-2.

The U-2 was an extremely advanced reconnaissance aircraft planned and produced amidst enormous secrecy by the Lockheed company. Powered by a Pratt & Whitney J57 engine with a newly-designed fuel system, the U-2 made its first flight in August 1955. The

U-2

single-seat plane had a remarkable capacity to fly at high altitudes and over great distances. Its long range was enhanced by glider-like wings that enabled the pilot to throttle down the engine and glide for long periods. Packed with information-gathering equipment and flying at very high altitudes where detection and interception were difficult or impossible, the U-2 was thought to be invulnerable.

However, the U-2 turned out to be both detectable and open to attack. On May 1, 1960, Francis Gary Powers, a civilian pilot working for the Central Intelligence Agency (CIA), was flying a U-2 over Soviet territory

when his aircraft was hit by a surface-to-air missile. Powers parachuted to safety, but was captured. An international incident resulted when the Soviet Union accused the U.S. of violating its air space and spying. At first the United States denied the charge; however, when the Soviet Union revealed it had captured Powers and publicly produced him, President Eisenhower was forced to admit he'd been flying for the U.S. government. Powers was sentenced to ten years in prison; two years later he was released in exchange for a Soviet spy.

The U-2 also played a major role in an international crisis that occurred in 1962. It was a U-2 aircraft that discovered Soviet offensive missile sites in Cuba and gathered photographic proof that these sites existed. In the ensuing dispute—called the Cuban Missile Crisis—the United States imposed a naval blockade of Cuba, and the confrontation between U.S. and Soviet ships at sea brought the two super-powers to the brink of war.

In addition to reconnaissance missions, U-2s have flown photography missions for the Federal Emergency Management Agency (FEMA) to help with disaster relief.

By the end of the 20th century, versions of the U-2 (the U-2R and U-2S) were powered by one Pratt & Whitney J75 engine and one General Electric F-118 engine that develop 17,000 pounds of thrust. They fly at faster than 475 mph, or Mach 0.58, and have a range that exceeds 7,000 miles.

90. Guppy
1962

When U.S. troops and cargo are sent overseas, men and equipment are often loaded aboard huge C-130 and C-147 cargo planes. However, these are not the largest cargo planes in the world. That distinction belongs to a mammoth aircraft called the Super Guppy.

With the advent of the U.S. space program came the problem of transporting enormous pieces of equipment. A California company named Aero Spacelines turned its attention to the task of transporting space program components, such as booster rockets, as well as carrying other oversize loads, including aircraft parts, equipment used in the oil industry, and cargo too large for even the biggest transport planes.

In 1961 Aero Spacelines began to convert a Boeing B-377 Stratocruiser to serve as a huge cargo plane. They extended the fuselage 16 feet, 8 inches in front of the wing and added height to the fuselage by creating a "bubble" that would permit the B-377 to accommodate cargo with a diameter of up to 9 feet, 9 inches. Thus they created the B-377PG, which was called the Pregnant Guppy. It first flew on September 19, 1962.

Beginning in the summer of 1963, the B-377PG was in service with NASA, carrying hardware for the space program. The Guppy has an "economic" cruising speed of 253 mph and a maximum cruising speed of 288 mph. It has a service ceiling of 25,000 feet, and its range—with a maximum **payload** and 45-minute fuel reserve—is 505 miles.

The larger B-377SG Super Guppy came next. An expanded version of the Pregnant Guppy, the Super Guppy has a longer wingspan and is powered by four 7,000-horsepower **turboprop engines**. It is 25 feet wide, 25 feet, 6 inches high, and its cargo

Super Guppy

compartment is 108 feet, 10 inches long.

The Super Guppy is vital to NASA; it's the only aircraft capable of carrying the third stage of a Saturn V launch vehicle and the Lunar Module adapter.

Since 1972, the Super Guppy has also been employed in Europe. Airbus Industries, which builds large-capacity airliners, uses four Super Guppies to carry Airbus assemblies from one production center to another. This version of the Super Guppy is designated the Guppy-201. It is as wide as the Super Guppy, but has an even greater cargo capacity. Its cargo compartment is 111 feet, 6 inches long, 25 feet, 1 inch wide, and 25 feet, 6 inches high. To make loading easier, the Guppy-201's forward fuselage and cockpit can be swung open 110 degrees.

While the "floating palaces" that transported ship passengers in luxury for much of the first half of the 20th century are now gone, there is still one great ocean queen that regularly sails back and forth across the Atlantic—the *Queen Elizabeth 2*, affectionately called the *QE 2*.

Built for the Cunard Line by Upper Clyde Shipbuilders at Clydebank, Scotland, the

QE2 under construction

QE2 was launched on September 20, 1967. Displacing 65,863 tons, she is 963 feet long and 105 feet across the **beam**. The *QE2* is powered by nine diesel turbine engines that generate 110,000 horsepower to drive two 350-ton electric motors and turn two six-bladed screws. She has the largest propulsion system built for a commercial ship and the largest electric motors in the world. Her cruising speed is 28 knots and her maximum speed is 32 knots. She has a **bulbous bow**, an incredibly strong **hull**, and her rudder weighs 80 tons.

The *QE 2* can accommodate more than 1,500 passengers and makes two types of trips: North Atlantic crossings, usually

between Southampton, England, and New York, and special holiday luxury cruises. She is operated and maintained by a crew of 1,000 women and men.

The *QE2* has made more than 1,000 Atlantic crossings and is one of the largest ships currently sailing the world's oceans. Her engines require 433 tons of fuel a day, and one gallon of fuel moves her less than 50 feet. Nevertheless, she is equipped with advanced navigation systems and an autopilot, and requires half as much fuel as the first *Queen Elizabeth*.

The *QE 2* was designed for safety, speed, and maneuverability. Her hull is subdivided into 15 watertight compartments. She has **bow thrusters** for easier control and two sets of fin stabilizers that can decrease a 20 degree roll to only 3 degrees. Her aluminum **superstructure** makes her a relatively light vessel and gives her a more shallow **draught**, so she can dock in many different types of ports all over the world. To ensure that she always has the power she needs, one of her engines is always closed down for routine maintenance.

The *Queen Elizabeth 2* was also designed for luxury. She has 13 decks, and her open deck space is the largest of any ocean liner. On board the *QE 2* are five restaurants, five bars and lounges, a theater, a library, a fitness center, and both outdoor and indoor swimming pools.

When people think of supersonic commercial airliners, the Concorde Supersonic Transport (SST) comes to mind. (However, the first supersonic transport to actually take to the air was the Russian Tupolev-144, which flew at supersonic speed on June 5, 1969; the aircraft stopped flying after a fatal accident on June 1, 1978.)

A joint project between England's British Aircraft Corporation and France's Sud-Aviation, the Concorde was the first SST to enter full service. The French prototype first flew on March 2, 1969; the English prototype on April 9, 1969. The plane was named Concorde to symbolize this international collaboration.

The Concorde has a cantilever, low-wing design with a large delta wing and a long, narrow **fuselage**. It is 203 feet, 9 inches long, and its wingspan is 83 feet, 10 inches. Its tail is simply a rudder and a vertical fin. Its landing gear consists of twin wheels near the nose and a four-wheel combination under each wing.

Concorde

Flown by a three-person crew, the Concorde is powered by four specially-developed Rolls Royce Olympus **turbojet** engines. It carries most of its 34,048 gallons of fuel in the wings, but there are also four fuselage tanks. The Concorde uses its fuel for two other purposes besides driving its engines. The fuel carried in the wings helps reduce wing temperature during supersonic flight. In addition, in flight, fuel is automatically transferred to different parts of the plane to maintain its center of gravity. The Concorde cruises at 1,354 mph, or Mach 2.04, at 51,300 feet and has a service ceiling of 60,000 feet. Its range is 4,090 miles.

One of the most well-known features of the Concorde is its distinctive hooked-nose. Because of its delta-wing configuration, the plane must be flown at a steep angle at low subsonic speeds. This gives the pilots a limited view of the ground when taking off and climbing, as well as when approaching a runway and during touchdown. This problem was solved by designing a front nose section that can be lowered to give the flight crew a better view. It's lowered 5 degrees for takeoff and 12.5 degrees for approach and landing.

The Concorde also has a retractable visor to protect its windscreen from the kinetic heat generated when cruising at supersonic speeds.

The Concorde carried passengers for the first time on January 21, 1976, when British Airways and Air France began regular service. Seating capacities vary with each airline; maximum passenger capacity is 144.

A superbly-crafted airplane, the Concorde is a source of great pride for England and France, but is viewed less enthusiastically by those who object to its noise and potential for polluting the environment.

AV-8B Harrier II

The Harrier is the first operational vertical and short take-off and landing (V/STOL) fighter. With the exception of the less sophisticated Yakovlev Yak-36 Forger, it is the only V/STOL combat plane in active service.

The Harrier is a high-performance fighter that can take off and land vertically, take off and land using a short runway area, and fly close to the speed of sound. Unlike other planes, it cannot be taken out of action by destroying its runways. In addition, it can be concealed—fully ready for combat—in a hangar, a cave, a forest, or dense city areas.

In 1957, Hawker Aircraft's Sir Sydney Camm and Dr. Stanley Hooker, working for Bristol Siddeley Engines, collaborated on a plane to be powered by Bristol's new **turbofan** engine, which came to be known as the Pegasus. The Pegasus was developed to provide jet-lift for vertical-takeoff fixed-wing craft. It accomplished this by discharging exhaust air through four nozzles, working in pairs, that could each be rotated more than 90 degrees to direct thrust down, to the rear, or in any direction in between.

Camm developed a compact, shoulder-wing **monoplane** flown by one pilot seated in the nose. On each side of the **fuselage** was a large semi-circular air intake. The landing gear consisted of a single nosewheel, twin main wheels, and a small retractable balancer wheel at the tip of each wing.

The Hawker P.1127 prototype made its first hovering flight on October 21, 1960. On September 12, 1961, it completed its first in-air changes between vertical and horizontal flight. By directing the engine thrust down, the plane achieved vertical lift; then the four nozzles were slowly turned toward the rear of the plane for forward thrust. When forward speed reached the point where the plane could be supported by wing-lift, the nozzles were turned completely to the rear of the plane. To land vertically, the pilot reversed this sequence. When hovering and during low-speed maneuvers, the plane was kept stable by small reaction control jets in the tail, nose, and wingtips.

In 1965 a pre-production version called the Kestrel underwent testing. Before the tests were even begun, the British government ordered six of the remarkable new planes. These aircraft were the first to be called Harrier. The first of these made its maiden flight on August 31, 1966. The Harrier became operational with the Royal Air Force on April 1, 1969 —the RAF's 51st birthday.

This unique, versatile fighter became the first foreign combat aircraft to be imported by the U.S. military for regular use. The Spanish navy also has a squadron of Harriers, which they call the Matador.

As commercial aviation developed, the major goals of airline companies—aside from improving safety records—were creating planes that flew faster and had larger capacities for passengers. The goal of a larger capacity was attained with Boeing's 747 "Jumbo Jet."

The 747 is so massive that the Boeing company built a new factory to produce it. No prototype was made; Boeing's demonstration model, which was unveiled on September 30, 1968, became the original production plane. The first flight took place on February 9,1969; regular service began on January 22, 1970, on Pan American's New York–London route.

The 747 is truly jumbo. It has the biggest body of all commercial passenger planes and is powered by four Pratt & Whitney JT9D **turbofan** engines with 50,000 lbs. of thrust each. When introduced in 1970, the JT9D was the most powerful and most efficient jet engine available for commercial airliners. The 747 has a maximum speed of 602 mph, a cruising ceiling of 45,000 feet, a fuel capacity of 47,210 gallons and a range of 5,980 miles. It can carry as many as 500 passengers, but airlines can earn a profit even when the plane flies empty, by filling its vast cargo bay.

The 747 has a low-wing configuration and carries its wing-mounted engines in pods. In addition to its size, it is best known for its wide-body, two-deck, "double-bub-

ble" **fuselage**. The flight deck is on the upper level, in the forward section of the plane's distinctive hump. The main passenger cabin runs the length of the fuselage, under the cockpit and all the way to the nose of the plane. The cabin is 20 feet, 1.5 inches wide, 185 feet long, and seats nine across. An upper-deck lounge accommodates 16 first-class passengers.

An extremely well-designed aircraft, this enormous plane can be flown by a three-person crew. Its flight controls are completely powered, and it can even make automatic landings.

Air traffic controllers welcomed the 747 because it had the potential to make their job easier. Two 747s could replace five to ten smaller planes. However, because each 747 can carry as many as 500 people—though 350 people is more common—they sometimes overwhelmed the passenger capacities of airports. If two 747s arrived simultaneously, 700–1,000 people might disembark all at once.

When the 747 was introduced, the airline industry resisted calling it a "Jumbo Jet." Industry people feared the public would associate the new plane with elephants, so the airline industry hoped the 747 would become known as the "Giant Jet." Whatever people called it, the Boeing 747 was a major advance in the increased capacity of commercial airliners.

747 piggybacking the Space Shuttle

The Grumman F-14 Tomcat represents modern military aircraft technology at its best. It has been called "unquestionably one of the finest warplanes in the world today."

The F-14 is termed a variable-geometry aircraft because the angle of its wings can be changed. The plane's wing sweep is controlled by a Mach sweep programmer that automatically adjusts the angle of the wings when taking off and landing on an aircraft carrier, while screaming through the sky in a dogfight, or on low-level attacks against ground targets.

The F-14 also has wing elements called glove vanes, which are automatically extended at supersonic speeds to keep the aircraft stable. Other control features include **spoilers**, **trailing-edge** flaps, and **leading-edge slats**. Amazingly adept at maneuvering, the Tomcat is constructed with titanium, boron-epoxy, and other composites that give it very solid structural integrity.

The F-14 was intended for duty on aircraft carriers. The first prototype was lost in a non-fatal accident on its first flight. The second prototype had its first successful flight on May 24, 1971, and flight testing then began. U.S. Navy contracts were awarded for 12 research and development aircraft, and the first F-14s entered service with the navy in October 1972.

The F-14 is flown by a two-man crew seated one behind another, and is powered by two 20,900-pound-thrust Pratt & Whitney afterburning **turbofan** engines. Afterburners increase the thrust of a jet engine by burning additional fuel with the residual oxygen in the hot exhaust gases. The Tomcat's cruising speed is 460–633 mph. It can fly as fast as 1,564 mph, or Mach 2.34, for a two-minute dash and at 1,432 mph, or Mach 2.17, for prolonged periods.

One of the Tomcat's main tasks is long-range air defense of ships. It's armed with air-to-air missiles that include the medium-range Sparrow and close-range AIM-9 Sidewinder, as well as a 20-mm mutli-barreled cannon for use in dogfights. For interception, it carries six Phoenix air-to-air missiles. (The Phoenix has a range of 124 miles, making it the longest-range air-to-air missile in use today.) With its ultra-sensitive, nose-mounted radar detection systems, the Tomcat can locate and attack an airborne target at a distance of 100 miles. As a low-level ground attack plane, the F-14 carries 14,500-pound bombs as well as other **ordnance**.

In 1992 a F-14A, modified to serve as a bomber and nicknamed the "Bombat," entered service with the aircraft carrier *John F. Kennedy*. The latest version of the Tomcat, the F-14D "Super Tomcat," has digital avionics and carries laser-guided smart bombs in addition to its Phoenix air-to-air missiles.

F-14 Tomcat

In 1963 the U.S. Air Force began considering a new type of strategy for dealing with the threats posed by the Cold War. This strategy revolved around aircraft that came to be labeled AWACS, which stood for Airborne Warning And Control System. Envisioned as electronic eyes and ears that would warn of an attack by manned or unmanned aircraft, AWACS would function as flying command centers that directed air activity during a conventional or nuclear war. To make this idea a reality, Boeing created the E-3A Sentry.

The E-3A Sentry is a modified Boeing 707. It is both a flying radar station resistant to signal jamming and a control, command, and communications center. Bristling with the most advanced communications equipment, AWACS aircraft can coordinate a country's entire combat response. They have long-range, high- and low-level surveillance ability in any kind of weather and over any kind of terrain, and they can stay airborne for more than eight hours without refueling.

To fulfill its new role, the 707 was refitted with four Pratt & Whitney **turbofan** engines that were increased to 21,000 pounds of thrust. Another change gave the AWACS plane its unique look—the large rotodome that sits 11 feet above the rear of the **fuselage**, supported by two wide struts. The rotodome has a diameter of 30 feet, a depth of 6 feet, and contains surveillance radar and antennae. When operating, it rotates at 6 rpm. When not in use, it continues to rotate at 1/24th this speed so that the low temperatures of the

plane's altitude don't harden the rotodome's lubricant, preventing operation. The E-3A also has antennae in its wings, fuselage, fin, and tail.

An AWACS aircraft is a complex flying communications center that requires not only a crew of four, but 13 to 19 AWACS specialists to operate all its equipment. This equipment includes multimode radar, an IBM high-speed computer, and a newly developed Joint Tactical Information Distribution

AWACS E-3A Sentry

System (JTIDS), which can provide high-speed communications for as many as 98,000 people. AWACS aircraft are built with intricate wiring and cooling systems, and have generators to provide the enormous amount of electrical power they require.

The E-3A began service on March 24, 1977. The AWACS were some of the first aircraft to be deployed in the 1991 Desert Storm war against Iraq, during which they flew more than 400 missions. Desert Storm marked the first time in the history of aerial warfare that an entire air war was recorded with video and reconnaissance cameras. It was the E-3A, with its enormous data-gathering capabilities and vast array of electronic equipment, that made this possible.

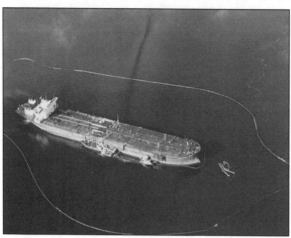

Exxon Valdez

Tankers are vessels specially constructed to carry liquid cargo. For seagoing tankers this cargo is usually oil, although some tankers carry liquefied natural gas. Tankers consist of a **hull** that has several single containers. Each container, or tank, runs the width of the ship. There is a narrow compartment between each tank that keeps them separate, so if the hull is penetrated a leak can be limited to that part of the ship.

The first tankers carried up to 5,000 tons of oil. The next generation of tankers carried 10,000 to 15,000 tons, but, as the 20th century progressed, the use and demand for oil thoroughout the world grew enormously. Tankers grew to keep pace.

By the late 1960s, very large crude carriers (VLCC) were being built. These ships carry 250,000–275,000 tons. Next came ultra large crude carriers (ULCC) that have capacity for 400,000 tons.

In 1989, one of these ULCC's—the super tanker *Exxon Valdez*—caused the worst oil spill in U.S. history—and one of the worst environmental disasters of the late 20th century. Shortly after midnight on March 24, the

Exxon Valdez ran aground on Bligh Reef in the upper part of Prince William Sound, Alaska. She was carrying about 53 million gallons of crude oil. Her hull was punctured, and in a few days almost 11 million gallons of oil spilled into Prince William Sound.

A great deal of the oil was not recovered, and the Alaskan government said that the spill took the lives of "tens of thousands of sea birds, hundreds of otters, dozens of bald eagles."This total did not include the thousands of animals that died because their habitat was damaged or destroyed. The oil eventually reached shorelines nearly 600 miles from the site of the spill, affecting areas that included a national forest, four national wildlife refuges, three national parks, five state parks, four state critical habitat areas, and a state game sanctuary.

An investigation into the disaster revealed that the ship's captain was negligent and he was held responsible; he was fired by the Exxon company, which then spent millions of dollars to help clean up the damage.

As a result of the *Exxon Valdez* spill, Congress passed the Oil Pollution Act of 1990. This law required that by 1994 all new tankers sailing in U.S. waters had to have double hulls, and that by 2010 all tankers in U.S. waters must have double hulls. In addition, tankers must have a Certificate of Responsibility for the oil in their holds, and they are liable for cleaning up any spills from their ships.

The *Exxon Valdez* was repaired, renamed the *Exxon Mediterranean*, and in 1990 returned to service, operating in the Persian Gulf.

Perhaps the most mysterious aircraft of modern times is the B-2 bomber, the technological wonder that is "invisible" to radar detection. The B-2 is an extremely controversial aircraft for two reasons: its enormous cost, and the fact that some critics question the claim that it is an undetectable, high-performance combat plane. The official name of this aircraft is the B-2 Spirit, but to the public it will probably always be known as the Stealth.

Design of the B-2 began in 1978, when the Air Force wanted an Advanced Technology Bomber (ATB) to replace the B-52. Originally envisioned as a high-altitude bomber, the B-2's design was later revised to include low-level missions. The B-2 flew for the first time on July 17, 1989, soaring over the California desert for 2 hours and 20 minutes. The plane then underwent such extensive testing that the first production aircraft (B-2A) wasn't delivered until December 1993.

The Stealth is still shrouded in secrecy, but some details have become available. The plane's frame has a honeycomb design and is made of radar-absorbent graphite/epoxy materials, as well as titanium and aluminum. The B-2 is shaped in a wide V; its **fuselage** blends with the center section of its wings, making it appear to be all one piece. The flight deck and **payload** area are in front of the wings' apex, and this section blends into the wings' upper surfaces.

The Stealth is flown by a two-person crew, seated side by side. Unlike other bombers, both crew members are pilots; there is no designated navigator or bombardier. There is also a station for a third pilot. The cockpit has a rounded windshield with a wire inside that helps disperse radar signals.

The B-2 is powered by four 19,000-pound-thrust General Electric nonafterburning **turbofan** engines mounted in pairs and set in the wing structure. It flies at a maximum speed of 545 mph above 40,000 feet, and 569 mph at sea level, and has a range of 5,300–6,600 miles, depending on altitude and bomb load.

The B-2 wasn't designed with fixed guns, but is equipped to carry nuclear weapons and a variety of conventional bombs. It also has the capability to deploy sea mines. It can carry a bomb load up to 40,000 pounds in two side-by-side bays that each has a rotary launcher assembly.

The Stealth's radar equipment includes very advanced low-probability-of-intercept radar that has 21 modes of operation. In addition, it has self-protective radar systems that help it elude enemy radar by emitting their own radar waves. Two paired air intakes, blended into the upper wing surface, help cool the engines to avoid detection by infrared heat-sensing equipment.

The cost of manufacturing each Stealth bomber is approximately $1.3 billion.

B-2 Stealth

Air Force One

Its official designation is VC-25A, but it's known as Air Force One—the aircraft that carries the president of the United States.

Any air force plane on which the president flies is given the radio call sign "Air Force One," but two are permanently designated as the "flying White House." These are specially-modified Boeing 747-200Bs carrying tail numbers 28000 and 29000.

Official air transport for the president began in 1944, when Franklin D. Roosevelt used a C-54 Skymaster, named the *Sacred Cow*. President Harry Truman traveled in a DC-6 called *Independence*, and President Dwight Eisenhower flew in a VC-121E Constellation called the *Columbine III*. Air Force One was first used as a call sign in September 1961, to identify the C-118 carrying President John F. Kennedy.

The most famous presidential plane is the C-137C, tail number 26000, that carried Kennedy on his ill-fated trip to Dallas on November 22, 1963, and returned his body to Washington, D.C. Lyndon B. Johnson took the oath of office to become the 36th U.S. president aboard this plane. In 1972, it flew President Richard Nixon on his historic trips to the People's Republic of China and the Soviet Union.

The first VC-25A, tail number 28000, took to the air as Air Force One on September 6, 1990. What makes this 747-200B different from the standard 747 is that it has been customized to meet the needs of the president and his staff. Once on board Air Force One, the president has everything necessary to stay in touch with the rest of the government, run the country, and command the U.S. military from the air.

Presidential accommodations include an office, a stateroom, and a dressing room. There are also a conference room and a dining room, as well as separate accommodations for staff, Secret Service and security officers, guests, and the news media. The plane can carry up to 102 people, including the crew. Two kitchens can provide as many as 100 meals at a time, and there is an area stocked with medical equipment.

Powered by four General Electric jet engines, each with 56,700 pounds of thrust, Air Force One can fly as fast as 701 mph and has a range of 9,600 miles. It is 231 feet, 10 inches long and has a wingspan of 195 feet, 8 inches.

Air Force One is operated by a crew of 26, which has its own rest area and kitchen. The members of the presidential air crew are assigned to Air Mobility Command's 89th Airlift Wing at Andrews Air Force Base, Maryland.

During World War II the aircraft carrier was the premier force at sea. Since that time, intercontinental ballistic missiles have become the ultimate offensive weapon, but carriers remain the central component of any modern navy. In the 1970s, the U.S. Navy introduced a program to create what is today the world's largest, most advanced warship—the nuclear-powered Nimitz class aircraft carrier. One of the latest Nimitz class carriers—and one of the largest warships in the world—is the *John C. Stennis*.

Designated CVN-74, the *John C. Stennis* was built in Newport News, Virginia. Christened on November 11, 1993, and commissioned on December 9, 1995, she displaces 97,000 tons and is 1,092 feet long. Her flight deck is 257 feet wide and comprises 4.5 acres. From **keel** to mast she is 244 feet high—as tall as a 24-story building. Her maximum speed is more than 30 knots.

The *John C. Stennis* has two nuclear reactors that drive four turbines generating 260,000 horsepower. These engines turn four screws that have five blades each. Each screw weighs 33.1 tons. Her two 30-ton anchors were originally on the *Forrestal* (see no. 86).

The *John C. Stennis* contains four aircraft elevators, four catapults, and four arresting gear engines which can slow landing aircraft. Her **air wing** is comprised of about 80 aircraft that include F/A-18 Hornets, F-14 Tomcats, EA-6B Prowlers, S-3 Vikings, E-2C Hawkeyes and SH-60 Seahawks. Her crew, including air wing personnel, numbers 6,200.

The carrier's onboard defenses include Sea Sparrow short-range surface-to-air missiles, the Phalanx Close-in Weapons System—an extremely rapid-firing six-barreled 20-mm gun for use against cruise missiles—and electronic decoys for use as countermeasures against missiles and torpedoes.

The *John C. Stennis* generates enough electricity to supply power to 2,000 homes. There are 2,000 telephones on the ship, over 900 miles of cable and wiring, and more than 30,000 light fixtures. Her cooks serve 18,600 meals a day. She carries about three million gallons of fuel for her aircraft and escort ships. The vessel also has numerous repair facilities that include an aircraft maintenance department and a micro-miniature electronics repair shop. If all of her technical manuals were stacked in a column, it would be as tall as the Washington Monument.

The *John C. Stennis* cost $3.5 billion to build and was designed to be in service for 50 years. By the end of the 1990s, there were eight Nimitz-class carriers in service, and one more under construction. The U.S. Navy planned to ultimately operate 12 of these extremely advanced "super-carriers."

A Nimitz class aircraft carrier

GLOSSARY

aft at or toward the rear of a ship or an aircraft

air wing an aircraft carrier's aircraft element

altimeter a navigational instrument that measures altitude

amidships middle of the ship

Automatic Direction Finder (ADF) a navigation system that allows pilots to use radio stations to determine position

avionics modern electronic systems and equipment used in aviation

backstay any of various shrouds that reinforce a ship's masts against forward pull

ballast tanks compartments that take in and expel water so submarines can submerge and return to the surface

battle stars the names of actions in which a ship has participated—usually publicly displayed

beam, abeam, across the beam measurement of the width of a ship

bilge keels projections on the side of a ship that are parallel to the keel and angled downward

biplane an airplane with two pairs of wings fixed at different levels

Blue Riband trophy given to passenger liners for the fastest Atlantic crossing

bonaventure mizzen fourth mast, set between the mizzen and main mast of a ship

bow the front of a vessel

bowsprit a spar (a support) projecting from the upper end of the bow of a sailing vessel

bow thrusters powered propeller or jet that moves a ship's bow sideways for easier control

brig a two-masted ship that carried square sails on both masts

bulbous bow a round, full ship bow shaped like a bulb

bulkhead a wall-like construction inside a ship or an airplane, used for forming watertight compartments or strengthening the structure

caravels small vessels used by the Spanish and Portuguese in the 16th century for trade and exploration, and generally used for trade throughout the Mediterranean during the 14-17th centuries

carronades very short, light, carriage-mounted guns that use a small charge to fire a heavy shell over a short distance

casemate fortified enclosure for artillery, usually made of iron

chronometer an accurate time-keeping device that enabled seamen—and later fliers—to determine their longitude and get a fix on their position

clinker-built overlapping planks on the side of the ship

close, to close ships engaging in battle at close quarters

compass (magnetic) instrument that indicates direction relative to the earth's magnetic poles

compass (sun) instrument that indicates direction relative to the position of the sun

conning tower armored pilot-house of a warship

cowlings removable metal coverings over an engine

dead reckoning estimating the position of a ship or aircraft by calculating the direction and distance traveled and comparing it to a previous position

dogfights aerial battles between fighter planes

double bottom space at the bottom of a ship that prevents it from sinking if the hull tears open

draught (also draft) the depth of water to which a vessel is immersed when bearing a given load

drift meter a navigational instrument that helps an airplane pilot say on course

ensign flag flown from a ship indicating nationality

flagship a ship that carries the commander of the fleet or division and carries his flag; also the main vessel of a shipping line

fore at or toward the bow of a ship or an aircraft

forecastle a house-like structure at the front of a ship originally built for security, later used for quarters

freeboard distance from the waterline of a ship to the upper deck

funnel smokestack

fuselage the central structure of an airplane, containing passenger and cargo compartments

hold large compartment below decks, used to carry cargo, provisions, and equipment

hull the hollow lowermost part of a ship floating partially submerged and supporting the remainder of the ship

hydrofoils winglike structures attached to a boat that raise all or part of the hull out of the water when the boat is moving, reducing drag

ironclads wooden ships with iron plating over their hulls keel a central fore-and-aft structural member in the bottom of a ship's hull

GLOSSARY

keel a central fore-and-aft structural member in the bottom of a ship's hull

knot measurement of speed equal to one nautical mile (6,080 feet) per hour

lateen triangle-shaped sail

leading edge front of an aircraft

leading-edge slats movable control surfaces on the front of an aircraft's wing

listing leaning

magazine place where ammunition is stored

military masts masts that carry signal lights, signal flags, aerials, and other modern equipment instead of sails

mizzen the most rear mast on a ship

monoplane an airplane with one set of wings

mothballed put into long storage for possible future use

ordnance military weapons with their equipment, ammunition, etc.

outriggers long, thin floats that help prevent boats from sinking

packet-ships, packets ships used to carry mail, cargo, and passengers on regular routes between two ports; during war, they were armed for defense

payload passengers and cargo that an aircraft carries

pontoons flat-bottomed boats; also, airplane floats used instead of wheels for water landings

poop deck partial deck above a ship's main afterdeck

rake forward angle of a ship's bow

range distance a ship or plane can travel before its fuel is exhausted

royal ensign flag with a special insignia indicating the ship was supported by royalty

run the shape of the rear part of the underbody of a boat, it determines how much resistance a ship encounters as it moves through the water; a "clean" run has less resistance, so the ship moves through the water faster

scurvy disease caused by a deficiency of vitamin C

scuttled deliberately sunk

sextant a navigational instrument that helps pilots determine their location by measuring the positions of the stars and planets

ships of the line ships deemed to have adequate weaponry to be in the line of battle

side-wheeler common paddle-wheel design with two paddles, one mounted amidships on each side of the boat

sloop a single-masted ship with sails on both the fore and aft sides of the mast

spar support used in the rigging of a ship

spoilers hinged plates on a plane's wing that increase lift and reduce drag

spiritsail a small sail set on the bowsprit to provide balance

starboard right side of a boat or an airplane

steerage large area below decks used for transporting poorer passengers who could not afford to pay for a cabin

stern the rear of a vessel

sterncastle house-like structure at the rear of a ship originally used for security

sternpost rear-most timber, attached to the keel

stern-wheeler common design of paddle-wheeler with one paddle mounted at the rear of the boat

stressed-skin smooth metal surface attached to an aircraft's frame

supercharger compressor that feeds air under high pressure to an engine's cylinders

superstructure constructions on a ship above the upper deck

swept-wing wings set on an angle to the fuselage

tail-gun turret round enclosure containing guns, mounted on the fuselage of an aircraft

three-mile limit point from land mass where international waters begin

throttle slowly give an engine more power

trailing edge rear end of an airplane

turbofan a turbojet engine in which a fan increases thrust by forcing air into the hot turbine exaust

turbojet jet engine with a turbine-driven compressor that develops thrust from the exhaust of hot gasses

turboprop jet engine with a turbine compressor that drives a propeller

variable pitch propeller allows pilots to change the speed of the propeller blades for different situations

Index

Index

Index